Man and Wife in Scripture

Man and Wife
in Scripture

by PIERRE GRELOT

Translated by ROSALEEN BRENNAN

 A COMPASS BOOK

LONDON : BURNS & OATES

Original edition "Le Couple Humain dans l'Écriture",
Éditions du Cerf, Paris.
Translated by Rosaleen Brennan

Nihil Obstat: Joannes M. T. Barton, S. T. D., L. S. S.
Censor deputatus

Imprimatur: † Georgius L. Craven, Epus. Sebastopolis, Vic. Gen.
Westmonasterii, die 17ª Martii, 1964

Catalogue No. 5/5957

PRINTED IN GREAT BRITAIN BY FLETCHER AND SON LTD, NORWICH,
AND BOUND BY RICHARD CLAY AND COMPANY LTD, BUNGAY, SUFFOLK, FOR
BURNS & OATES LIMITED, 25 ASHLEY PLACE, LONDON, S.W.1

CONTENTS

PREFACE

THE PRESENT work makes no claim to be a complete treatment of the biblical theology of marriage. Its aim is more limited. In justification of its limitations I feel it is perhaps advisable to give some account of its origins. The stimulus for it came from a talk given during a study conference for moral theologians. The organizers of the conference rightly thought it insufficient to consult only doctors, psychologists and historians when a full elucidation of the question of the human couple was required. It was no less important to study the biblical sources of the doctrine. For this reason the focal point of my lecture was not marriage itself seen as a whole but the human couple as it is portrayed in Scripture. The article was first published in an expanded form in the *Supplément de la Vie Spirituelle* (no. 57, 1961, pp. 135–98).

It is in this form that I would have left it but for Père Chifflot's kind encouragement to revise it for a volume in the "Lectio Divina" series. Two solutions were open to me: either to develop the original study by commenting in detail on the scriptural texts on which it was based, or to retain the synthetic character while sacrificing completeness. I chose the second solution. Theologians looking for detailed analyses can always consult the many biblical commentaries. It seemed worthwhile, therefore, to provide a wider public with an account of some hundred pages rather than to discourage potential readers by imposing three hundred pages upon them. The interest of any synthesis on a theological subject lies in its success in assembling, in a concise and accessible form, the essential elements of a problem which fuller treatises often only submerge beneath a mass of lengthy analyses obscuring their meaning. Since I have chosen to offer a synthesis, I can only hope my readers will excuse my not examining in detail every aspect of the theology of marriage. What I have done is to revise the article which appeared in *Supplément de la Vie Spirituelle,* expanding some pages, rewriting others which seemed to me less successful, and adding a few notes in support of my exegetics. It is common knowledge that a work of exegesis worthy of the name cannot dispense with the learned apparatus of footnotes and bibliography without losing its claim to be a serious study. The author is under an obligation to point out to his readers important further works of reference which would advance their knowledge of the subject; this does not necessarily mean that he has read them all himself. It will be immediately evident that my learned apparatus is irregular: there are many places where my contentions remain unsupported by famous names! I admit willingly that this makes it only half a serious study.

My fellow-exegetes may perhaps still reproach me with not having adhered to the form of biblical theology as they understand it: an "objective" study of "explicit" statements contained in the texts, which does not go beyond the limits of the literal meaning as it is understood by biblical criticism. Although I am aware of the necessity for rigorous criticism of the text, I am equally convinced that theological thought must advance beyond such naked results. These provide only the raw materials, which then require interpretation and synthesis in terms of the more general view which revelation as a whole gives us. I did not wish to limit myself merely to listing the views of the Jahvist historian, the author of the Proverbs, Ben Sirach, St. Paul and others on the human couple, fragmenting Scripture under the pretext of respecting the individuality of the authors. I have tried, therefore, to work out in the form of a reasoned analysis the problematic of the couple as it is presented to us in the Bible as a whole. Both the background of comparative religion, against which revelation has to be seen, and the findings of modern psychology have been useful in this task. It is certainly impossible for exegesis to interpret biblical texts correctly without putting them in the wider context of the ancient East; yet the real work of theology is to provide the link between divine revelation and human problems, as they are in any given age. It is these two demands which I have tried to satisfy. It may perhaps seem that, in fact, I have answered neither completely, but I did not aspire to do more than contribute one small stone to the great work of theology, which today is once again taking up the thorough study of fundamental problems, founding it on the results of a renewed biblical theology.

INTRODUCTION

WE SHOULD not expect to find in Holy Scripture an analysis of the human couple such as is given by modern writers. The Bible does not provide us with a detailed psychological examination of passionate love, as our playwrights and novelists do; nor with a philosophical treatise on the significance of love, such as we find in Plato's *Symposium;* nor, *a fortiori,* with a psychoanalytical study laying bare the mechanics of the instincts, their evolution, their disturbances and so on. It goes beyond such fragmentations and offers us a doctrine capable of integrating them. For it considers human sexuality as a whole and from a far more fundamental angle than those to which psychoanalysis, psychology or even metaphysics are committed: that of the relationship of the human couple with the living God.

It is, therefore, not merely a question of looking for a sexual ethic in Scripture. Such an ethic certainly exists, but it is totally dependent upon a far more general philosophy of life, outside which it loses its meaning. This doctrine is not the outcome of rational thought, tentative and necessarily limited in its affirmations as soon as it touches upon the mystery of God. It is itself the Word of God; it is part of revelation in the same way as the Trinity, christology, or the redemption. It is true that it never loses touch with the realities of human experience, but it treats of them only to illuminate them and, when necessary, to correct them by putting them into perspective as part of the mystery of salvation. Like everything which plays a rôle in human existence, sexuality is part of a universe created by God, fallen through man's offence, redeemed by the divine mercy. Because of this, it is the focal point of three forces: the force by which creation tends towards the end destined for it by the creator, the force of sin which separates it from this end and moreover divides it within itself, the force of grace which restores order and draws it back towards God by integrating it into the mystery of Christ.

It is this – the human couple's situation in life – which accounts for the fact that they are subject to a twofold stress. There is in the first place the tension between a certain ideal, of which they are vaguely aware in the sphere of their dreams, and the reality of their actual life with its unhappinesses and failures: it is impossible for them not to have the dream, but it belongs to the unattainable realm of paradise lost. The second tension is a creative one: that between the same delusive reality of everyday life and the new ideal which it is God's will to reconstruct by means of his light and his grace. In the sacrament which is their foundation and sanctification, the couple find not only the order and meaning of their existence but the power to translate it into real terms, for their link with the mystery of Christ gains them entry into the realm of paradise regained. In this world it is clearly impossible that they should escape altogether the hardships of the human condition, but since that time when Christ on the cross took upon himself the human burden, all suffering has become a means of redemption and it is in accepting the cross that the couple too attain paradise regained and enter into that new universe which the risen Christ has ready for mankind after its renewal.

This is the broad view which the Bible offers us. It scarcely need be said that this teaching will not be found set forth exactly in this form and completely developed in every one of the sacred books. In this respect, as in all the others, revelation has been given to man only in a progressive form and we have to wait for the New Testament to find it expounded in its entirety. Even in the Old Testament, however, we see it take a firm stand on essential principles and adopt a general form which is completely in keeping with its subsequent Christian flowering. And this later development of revelation is the more intelligible, the more precisely we know and understand the slow genesis which preceded and prepared the way for it during the centuries when God educated his people for Christ. It is for this reason that we are here going to trace step by step the history of this revelation in the three distinct stages of its evolution:

1. The fundamental data of the biblical revelation, put forward by the Old Testament in conscious reaction to the religious thought of the oriental environment.

2. The development of these data through successive stages of the Old Testament.

3. Their final flowering in the New Testament.

I

BASIC DATA

On the subject of the human couple, as on all others, the biblical revelation should not be seen in isolation. The cultural and religious environment, within which it has its place, possessed its own conception of human sexuality in its various aspects (love, fecundity, the institution of marriage). Considered in relation to this conception, the thought of the Old Testament shows points both of agreement and of divergence. It is in examining these more closely that we can arrive at a just appreciation of the fundamental claims of Scripture.

1. The Sacral Character of Sexuality in the Ancient East

Here we must first of all mention the findings of sociology. In ancient Eastern civilizations the matrimonial institution, which provides the framework for the human couple, has aspects which are notably different from those of the Christian conception of marriage. This need not, however, detain us for long, since the originality of the biblical doctrine, in contrast with those of the pagan civilizations which surrounded it, is far less on the sociological plane than on a strictly religious one. We will delimit the problem more from the standpoint of the history of religions.

The religions in question are above all those of the environment with which the people of the Bible had intimate links: the religions of Mesopotamia, Syria and Canaan; to a lesser degree, that of Egypt; as for those of Persia and Greece they only affected Hebrew thought at a relatively late period after biblical doctrine had already taken shape.[1] It is, moreover, pointless to examine in isolation each of the cults which could provide us with data. In Mesopotamia, Syria and Canaan there was practised a general syncretism, the spirit of which can be seen in Greece too. This means that on our particular subject we find the same general characteristics everywhere with only superficial variations. In short, even in those countries in which marriage is essentially a civil institution (as is the case in Mesopotamia), religious thought hallows human sexuality and everything connected with it by the two classic means of myth and ritual.

a. Myths

The importance of myths in ancient religions scarcely needs

[1] General works on the subject: J. Vandier, *La religion égyptienne,* series "Mana", 1, I: E. Dhorme, *Les religions de Babylonie et d'Assyrie,* "Mana", 1, II; R. Dussaud, *Les religions des Hittites et des Hourrites, des Phéniciens et des Syriens,* "Mana", 1, II; C. Picard, *Les religions préhelléniques,* "Mana", 2, I. — M. Brillant and R. Aigrain, *Histoire des religions,* vol. III: La religion égyptienne, by E. Drioton; La religion des préhellènes, by P. Demargne; vol. IV, Les religions asianiques, by M. Rutten; Le groupe assyro-babylonien, by R. Largement; Le groupe hébreu, by R. Largement. — M. Gorce and G. Mortier, *Histoire générale des religions,* vol. I. — But the useful information is scattered throughout these works. Translations of the relevant religious texts are to be found in the collec-

emphasis.[2] They constitute the highest form of their thought. They are, however, far from being simply the concrete, dramatic expression of rational thought, which is as yet incapable of being translated into abstract speculative terms.[3] Their value is an existential one. Into them ancient man projects his whole experience of life: his experience of social relationships, of relationships with the cosmic forces, of relationships with the divinity. These three aspects of human experience blend inextricably into one another, at a time when no qualitative distinction is made between the divine and the forces of the cosmos or the powers that govern human society.

These stories about deities[4] have their roots in a primordial age, anterior to, yet contemporaneous with, all human eras, and so reflect both the natural world as it is seen by man and the society in which he lives. Or, to put it more exactly, they constitute a world of archetypes, of which both nature and society show us more or less imperfect imitations.[5] The things of the universe

tion by J. B. Pritchard, *Ancient Near Eastern Texts Relating to the Old Testament* (Princeton, 1955).

[2] J. Henniger, *Le mythe en ethnologie,* art. *Mythe, Supplément au Dictionnaire de la Bible,* vol. VI, col. 225–46; M. Éliade, *Patterns in Comparative Religion* (London, 1958), pp. 410-34.

[3] The myth includes this element too: "Myth expresses in action and drama what metaphysics and theology define dialectically" (M. Éliade, *op. cit.,* p. 418). Cf. also H. Frankfort, *The Intellectual Adventure of Ancient Man* (Cambridge, 1947), p. 7.

[4] The definition of the myth as a "story about gods" is not unanimously accepted; cf. J. McKenzie, "Myth and the Old Testament" in *CBQ,* 1959, pp. 273–4. But, by any hypothesis, "stories about gods" belong to the category of myths.

[5] The term archetype evokes in itself an entire mental universe on which our conscious thought draws. It is at this point that the study of

and of history owe their intelligible significance and, ultimately, existence to the degree in which they reproduce this archetypal world, for it is only thus that they participate in its being.[6] Their connection with the archetypes also ensures their sacral nature: every action has a sacral value which reflects a divine activity. Inversely, if a sacral value is attributed to some human action or some cosmic force, then it has its archetype in the world of the gods. Thus the stories of gods found in mythology cannot be regarded as the gratuitous inventions of the imagination. If the "mythopoetic" function of man's mind makes use of the imaginative powers, it is for extremely serious purposes. Here a comparison might not unreasonably be made with the myths used by Plato as a starting-point for subsequent philosophic thought.[7]

comparative religion touches psychoanalysis. C. G. Jung and C. Kerényi in *Introduction to a Science of Mythology* (London, 1951) have attempted a systematic interpretation of the themes of the divine child and the mysteries of Eleusis using psychoanalytical methods. It goes without saying that in this book the idea of the archetype is developed in terms of Jungian psychoanalysis. The sense in which we are using it here is independent of this systematization.

[6] M. Éliade, *The Myth of the Eternal Return* (London, 1955), pp. 3–48; and *Patterns of Comparative Religion*, pp. 410–34.

[7] Clearly there is the fundamental difference that in Plato the myth is a learned device, which he uses deliberately to illustrate abstract ideas he later expounds more fully. In other respects the archetypal universe of the myths bears a strong resemblance to the world of the Platonic 'Forms', of which our world is an image or shadow, an imperfect imitation of the essential realities in the other eternal and unchanging world. This conception, elaborated philosophically by Plato, is one common to all the ancient religions and underlies their mythologies. Cf. M. Éliade, *The Myth of the Eternal Return*, p. 34. This has already been commented on by T. Gomperz, *Les penseurs de la Grèce*, vol. II (Paris, 1905), pp. 414f.

17

Within such a framework of thought human sexuality (which in itself possesses a sacral value) finds at the level of the myth the deepest source and justification of its sacral nature, the real principle of its meaning for man. Here the divine is not concentrated in a unique and personal God, completely transcendent by comparison with the actual realities of human experience. It is dispersed among a quantity of secondary figures, gods and goddesses, who themselves are or can form couples; as archetypes these couples are the concrete expression, each in their own way, of the various aspects of the man-woman relationship: fecundity, love, the marriage institution.

To deal first with the aspect of fecundity: procreation is here closely connected with the idea of creation and in many ancient languages the same word is used for both acts.[8] Underlying the different tales we find again and again the figures of the god-father and goddess-mother, the source of universal life, either in the world of the gods or in the natural world of vegetation, animals and humans.[9] The goddess-mother,[10] archetype of the Mother,

[8] Hebrew provides examples of this: the verb *banah* (to construct) which in Gen. 2:22 describes the creative act is connected etymologically with *ben* (son); the verb *qanah* can mean "create" (Gen. 14:19) or "procreate" (Gen. 4:1); the verb *bara* (the technical expression for "to create") is cognate with the Aramaic *bar* (son).

[9] Sumerian mythology, the oldest for which we possess textual evidence, gives prominence to the divine couple, the progenitors; they are Enki, god of the Ocean, and Ninhursag, the Earth-Mother, also called Nin-Ton, 'child-bearing woman'. See M. Lambert in *La naissance du monde, Sources orientales,* I (Paris, 1959), pp. 108-10; also S. N. Kramer in J. B. Pritchard, *Ancient Near Eastern Texts,* pp. 38-40.

[10] M. Éliade, *Patterns of Comparative Religion,* pp. 239-64; *Myths, Dreams and Mysteries* (London, 1960), pp. 155-89. See the magnificent *Hymn to the Earth* of the *Atharva Veda* in L. Renou, *La poésie religieuse de l'Inde*

personifies the earth, which engenders vegetation, and it is clear that all animal and human maternity derives from hers. The god-father who makes her fertile, archetype of the Father, is a heavenly god generally associated with the phenomenon of the storm,[11] for rain is as it were the fertilizing sperm which causes the germination of the plants in the womb of the earth-mother; again, all human and animal paternity is derived from his. As an extension of this elementary representation, the divine Father-Mother couple can undergo secondary variations. We have an example of this in the pantheon of the Canaanites of Ugarit, where we find in the chief place the god El,[12] ancestor of all the gods, "creator (or progenitor) of creatures",[13] "creator (or progenitor) of heaven and earth".[14] In the myth he is represented as fertilizing two wives who give birth to two sons, Dawn and Nightfall.[15] In any case it is here that human (and animal)

---

antique (Paris, 1942), pp. 38–44; Hymnes spéculatifs du Véda (Paris, 1956) pp. 189-202. J. Przyluski, La grande déesse (Paris, 1950) — although the author's thesis, that the cult of the Mother-Goddess is the starting-point of all religious phenomena, is highly debatable. E. O. James, The Cu t of the Mother-Goddess (London, 1959).

[11] M. Éliade, Patterns of Comparative Religion, pp. 86-91.

[12] M. H. Pope, El in Ugaritic Texts (Leiden, 1955).

[13] Literally bânê banâwât, "builder of things built" or "procreator of things procreated" (cf. note 8).

[14] In Gen. 14:19 the epithet qoneh shamaijn wa-'arets is used of El Elyon, the god of Melchisedech; the title is also found in Phoenician and even Hittite inscriptions. See A. Caquot, "La naissance du monde selon Canaan" in La naissance du monde, pp. 179f.

[15] Part of the text has been translated by M. H. Pope, op. cit., pp. 37–9; C. H. Gordon, Ugaritic Literature (Rome, 1949), pp. 57-62; R. Largement, La naissance de l'Aurore, poème mythologique de Ras Shamra-Ugarit (Gembloux – Louvain, 1949).

sexuality, as a fecund power, finds its archetype and, at the same time, the source of its sacral nature, its meaning, its purpose.

The man–woman relationship has a second aspect: passionate love (using "passionate" in a psychological and not in a moral sense, which usually has pejorative overtones). Here, too, we find in mythology the god- and goddess-lover, who are not necessarily identical with the god-father and goddess-mother. The goddess-lover epitomizes the sexual attraction which woman uses to seduce man and which gives her power over her partner or, rather, partners, for she often has many. Ishtar, the Babylonian counterpart of Venus or Aphrodite,[16] has for her chief lover Tammouz, god of vegetation, who dies and comes to life again as nature does in the course of its seasonal cycle.[17] But she also has many other passionate affairs. In the Gilgamesh epic the hero, whom she tries in vain to seduce, enumerates ironically the long list of her lovers followed by as many desertions: besides Tammouz, there is the dappled shepherd-bird, the stallion, the lion, the keeper of the herd, and her father's gardener ...,[18] an instructive list, which shows us this archetype of the woman-lover as the type of the seductive woman known to both gods and mortals. Nonetheless, it is in this myth of the goddess-lover that love,

[16] For Ishtar, see E. Dhorme in "Mana" 1, II, pp. 67–8.

[17] For the myth and its context, see G. Contenau, *Le déluge babylonien, Ishtar aux enfers, La tour de Babel* (Paris, 1952), pp. 123–225; E. A. Speiser in Pritchard, *Ancient Near Eastern Texts,* pp. 106–9. The myth also occurs in Sumerian mythology: S. N. Kramer, "Inanna's Descent to the Nether World" in Pritchard, *op. cit.,* pp. 52–7.

[18] The Gilgamesh Epic, tablet VI, 22–79 in A. Heidel, *The Gilgamesh Epic and Old Testament Parallels* (Chicago, 1946), pp. 50–2; E. A. Speiser in Pritchard, *op. cit.,* p. 84; P. Dhorme, *Choix de textes religieux assyro-babyloniens* (Paris, 1907), pp. 245–9.

both as an emotion and as a physical desire, finds an intrinsic justification and hallowing, regardless of the social conditions among which it arises: all male lovers live within the powerful aura of Ishtar, Aphrodite or Venus; it is her presence that they find in every woman for their joy or misery, since love brings alternately salvation and death.

To these two categories of myths which are concerned with fecundity and passion, we must add those which relate a divine marriage, the archetype of all weddings. It is in this form that we have in Ugaritic texts the story of a myth of Hurrite origin which describes the marriage of Nikkal (the Sumerian Nin-Gal or Great Lady) and the moon-god.[19] In this account, which is typical of its kind, the primordial couple, god-father and goddess-mother, do not even appear. This is quite simply because every marriage sees the girl passing from her father's to her husband's power.[20] On the other hand, the nuptial union of the god-bridegroom and his bride may have as its hero the national god of a city, an incarnation of political power and archetype of the king, as in the case of the Babylonian god, Marduk.[21]

The above enumeration of the mythical archetypes connected with sexuality is sufficient to show their close relationship with primitive polytheism. The ancients imagined a divine society

[19] C. H. Gordon, *Ugaritic Literature*, pp. 63–5; J. Gray, *The Legacy of Canaan* (Leiden, 1957), pp. 180–1; A. van Selms, *Marriage and Family Life in Ugaritic Literature* (London, 1954) pp. 35–44.

[20] Vedic literature too possesses a long poem, both mythical and ritual, which tells of the marriage of Soma with Sûryâ, the daughter of the Sun-god. See L. Renou, *Hymnes spéculatifs du Veda*, pp. 81–90.

[21] E. Dhorme in "Mana", 1, II, pp. 139–50 (marriage pp. 146f.).

21

modelled on human society. They projected on to that society the various elements of a sexual experience which oscillated between preoccupation with fecundity, an instinctive hallowing of everything which touched upon life, the anxiety to stabilize marriage as an established institution protected by the authority of society, and the impulsive overflowing of an eroticism which was more or less anarchic. All this is clearly present in the myths and it accounts for the sort of disassociation which is found in them between the essential aspects of sexuality. Marriage, love, and fecundity are not systematically united in one ideal couple who would serve as a model for every human couple. Each aspect is hallowed separately, so to speak, although there are certain obvious normal connections, such as that between marriage and fecundity. All this denotes a philosophical stage in which the different aspects of sexuality are not yet integrated into the vital union of an institution like that of Christian marriage, which provides a unique framework for morally good love and fecundity. The sexual ethic of such an ideology could not conceivably have as a basis the sort of hierarchy of values to which the Christian gospel has accustomed us.

b. Rites

It is commonly accepted that in the ancient religions myths and rites are very closely connected (although there are myths which have no ritual counterpart and rites which have no known mythical source).[22] Myths hallow the things of this world by

[22] This close correspondence of myth and ritual was given considerable emphasis by the contributors to the volume *Myth and Ritual,* published in 1933 by S. H. Hooke, which initiated renewed interest in the subject. For the most recent position see the contributions of S. H. Hooke and

providing a background of divine archetypes for them. Rites similarly hallow them but in an active way by establishing a real link, not merely an ideal one, between the earth and the world of the gods. In the cult man carries out certain actions, plays certain rôles and in doing so he is taken up into the sacred sphere of the divine. Some of these rites are in fact simply the reproduction, in a dramatic form preferably, of the exemplary action of the gods as it is described in the appropriate myth. The rites have their liturgy, established by usage, for which the myth provides what might be called the metaliturgy. In carrying them out in accordance with the established formulae, man has the intention of uniting himself with the action of the gods: in re-enacting this divine action, he makes it part of his life and benefits from its creative efficacity. This is especially true in the case of sexual rites, intended to hallow human sexuality as well as to ensure the influence of the gods on the fecundity of the animals and the fertility of the plants, both important factors in the lives of predominantly pastoral and agricultural peoples.

Here too, as in the case of the myths, a certain disassociation is apparent between the various aspects of sexuality. In the agrarian cultures,[23] built up on the fertility of the soil and the fecundity of the flocks, the hierogamy or divine marriage is often the object of a solemn celebration at the New Year. Nor is this merely a matter of a symbolic ceremony: the divine marriage is effectively re-enacted by the king, the official representative of the whole city, and a priestess chosen for the

S. G. F. Brandon in *Myth, Ritual and Kingship* (Oxford, 1958), pp. 1–21 and 261–91; see also E. O. James, *Myths and Rites in the Ancient Near East* (London, 1958).

[23] M. Éliade, *Patterns in Comparative Religion*, pp. 331–366.

occasion.[24] This is no purely commemorative and gratuitous operation. It is an act of sympathetic magic. By re-enacting in this world, in the sacred sphere of the cult, the archetypal sexual union of the god-father and goddess-mother (or of the god of vegetation and the goddess of love), it is intended to stimulate the fecundating forces of nature or the male sexual powers (human or animal) to imitation and thus to the fulfilment of their function of inseminating their partners. In this way it is thought to ensure both the success of the seasonal cycles which regulate the natural and animal worlds and the effective fecundity of human couples.

Outside this hierogamy which belongs to the cult of the city and which provides for the general interests of the whole community, the cult of the goddess-lover has as an essential part of its proceedings the sexual union of men with ritual prostitutes (sometimes male prostitutes, generally castrated) in the service of the goddess.[25] This rite should not be judged in the light of our moral standards but according to its religious purpose. The inmates of the sanctuaries are, moreover, by no means to be equated with those women in all civilizations who sell their services to pleasure-seeking men. On the contrary, they fulfil a function

[24] The classic case is that of the cult of Marduk at Babylon. Cf. H. Frankfort, *Kingship and the Gods* (Chicago, 1948), pp. 330–1. R. Largement in the article "Nouvel An en Mésopotamie" in *Supplément au Dictionnaire de la Bible,* vol. VI, col. 582–4 and in Brillant-Aigrain, *Histoire des religions,* vol. IV, pp. 131–5. For an earlier epoch S. N. Kramer gives two "love-songs" which have as their ritual setting the New Year hierogamy in Sumer in *History begins at Sumer* (London, 1961), pp. 299–303; cf. also Pritchard, *op. cit.,* p. 496.

[25] E. Dhorme in "Mana" 1, II, pp. 211–13; J. Bottero, *La religion babylonienne* (Paris, 1952), p. 113.

regarded as especially worthy of esteem: the same one that the goddess of love herself fulfils on the divine plane. Sexual union with these dedicated persons is a rite which is carried out inside the confines of the goddess' sanctuary. What is sought in this rite is a true religious integration of sexuality, an efficacious hallowing, the influence of which will be felt on every subsequent sexual act. It is as if, in uniting themselves with these ritual prostitutes, the men among the faithful were bringing about a real renewal of their own genital powers, intimately united with the divine power which is their principle[26] and which is realized through their sacred lovers. The efficacy of their action naturally extends too to the flocks and to the fertility of the soil. Here we see that the private interests of the shepherds and farmers play a decisive rôle in the cultic practices and are of far more importance than any motive of lust. It is probable that in a certain number of cases the operation of sympathetic magic underlying these rites went as far as acts of bestiality; nonetheless, these too were carried out not for their own sake but for the same purpose.[27]

Finally we must note those marriage rituals which consciously imitate the archetypal marriage of the gods. There is most evidence in the case of royal marriages, since the god of a city

[26] In a civilization completely different and distant from that of the biblical environment, Hindu tantrism retains certain sexual practices in which the believer tries to enter into union with the *cakti*, the vital feminine energy which represents the creative principle. An example is given in Renou, *Anthologie sanskrite* (Paris, 1947), p. 183. Here Indian thought has built on an ancient mythico-ritualistic basis common to all cults of the generative powers, which are found from the Mediterranean to India.

[27] This is the reason for the biblical prohibitions to be discussed later.

25

or an empire may to some extent be personified in its king.[28] Examples also exist, however, in the case of marriages between ordinary citizens.[29] The fact that these are, in addition, dependent upon the civil law does not prevent the mythical background from exerting its influence on the actual conception of the marriage institution, which is itself essentially sacred. But here sociology clearly interferes with religion: the rules governing the institution (including polygamy, divorce, concubinage, etc.) cannot all by any means be equated with the principles of the archetype, which is the mythical counterpart of the institution, although it is certainly true that as mythologies grow more complex, they introduce polygamy, divorce and concubinage into the world of the gods and in this way make it into an exact reflection of the world of mortals.

We have given here an outline of the religious environment

---

[28] In Egypt the king is completely identified with Horus, son of Osiris. The king and the queen-mother as a couple, therefore, incarnate the corresponding divine couple. Cf. H. Frankfort, *op. cit.*, pp. 36–45 (who emphasizes the complexity of the royal myth in Egypt). The king's principal wife is regarded as "daughter of the god" and among her titles are those of "wife of the god, mother of the god". Cf. A. Erman and H. Ranke, *La civilization égyptienne,* translated from the German (Paris, 1952), p. 104.

[29] This mythical background to ordinary marriages has survived in the Mandaean sect. Cf. E. S. Drower, *Sharh dQabin dShishlam Rba, Explanatory Comment on the Marriage-Ceremony of the Great Shishlam* (Rome, 1950). The Vedic poem cited in note 20 gives formulae to be observed in the celebration of any marriage. For the marriage ritual practised by the *Sûtras,* see L. Renou, *Anthologie sanskrite,* pp. 49–53. Of particular interest is the formula pronounced by the bridegroom: "I am he, you are she; I am Heaven, you are Earth . . . Come, we will marry and create children" (p. 50).

in which the biblical revelation will take place. It holds considerable interest for us, in that it shows the conception of sexuality and the couple towards which mankind spontaneously tends, when it is trying to hallow this aspect of life and integrate it into religion. To be fair, it is important to acknowledge that some positive values were very clearly appreciated in the pre-biblical era. It is no mean achievement to attribute a sacred character to everything which touches life, sex, and fecundity; to attempt to relate this important sphere of existence to the higher powers – or the one Power – on which it depends; to surround the use of the reproductive powers with a network of ritual rules and prohibitions to protect it from profanation; to establish laws making the family a social institution. Nonetheless, even these efforts quickly end in relapse, for they come up against limitations which make failure inevitable. The ethic which they establish remains at the juridical and ritual levels and is incapable of passing beyond what Bergson called "la morale close", a limited morality, incapable of snatching human love from the perils which threaten it and so allowing it to be realized in its true fullness. The myths and rites which act as support to this ethic canonize a situation in which the family group compromises with practices far removed from any ideal worthy of a couple's aspiration (polygamy, for example), while custom and even religion approve sexual aberrations which are an even greater departure from the ideal (ritual prostitution, homosexuality, even bestiality).

It would not be difficult to show that the neo-pagan world of today is going back, as it were instinctively, to this conception of things. Whether it tries to strip sexuality of its religious aura and reduce it to the rôle of a psycho-physiological

27

function[30] or whether it reconstructs around it a sort of mythology which hallows the blind forces of the instincts in a different way,[31] it manages to find a host of justifications for its actions. It is by no means certain that the sensual climate of fertility cults was more degrading than the latent eroticism into which the western world has plunged. And are we to maintain that the spiritual standards of a society the rites of which are characterized by the desire for fecundity are lower than one practising its voluntary limitation? This question does not, however, come within the scope of our investigation. Our purpose was simply to survey the ideological background against which the biblical revelation unfolded.

2. Biblical Revelation

We can now place the biblical conception of life in its proper perspective. First of all, we will obtain a general view by examining closely two texts which to some extent provide us with a synthesis: the two accounts of the creation of man. In them we have, in the guise of a concrete presentation, abstract ideas on

[30] This is a result of the rationalizing tendency of the modern world. Its most radical manifestation is perhaps the basic materialism from which certain Freudian movements have developed. Marx's position is subtler: it is possible to see in it a sort of latent sacralization. Cf. J. Y. Calvez, *La pensée de Karl Marx* (Paris, 1956), pp. 402–3, 511–12.

[31] Here the popular press and the cinema are principally responsible. It is easy to discern in both mythical themes capable of infinite variation, mythical heroes in innumerable reincarnations. Greco-roman antiquity gave a personal name to Aphrodite and Eros; but the truest form of cult is surely the unconditional surrender to their power, the submission to an absolute *libido*, that we see today.

the origin of sexuality and the source of sacrality which, in the proper perspective of biblical thought, play a rôle analogous to those myths which we have just analysed.

a. Break with the Religious Thought of the East

What is immediately striking about the biblical world as far as our subject is concerned are not the sociological modifications made in the institution of marriage.[32] On the contrary, accounts which have come down to us from the patriarchal epoch, as well historical documents and legal texts, presume or sanction a common law practically identical with that of neighbouring civilizations. We find polygamy, legalized concubinage, divorce and so on.

In contrast, there is a radical break with the ideological and ritual background which was the basis of the hallowing of sex in the pagan cults. And this is no belated or secondary development in the Jewish religion, but a direct consequence of its most fundamental tenets. Jahveh, the God of the Fathers who revealed his name to Moses (Exod. 3:13–15), who led Israel out of Egypt to make her his people, who demands from her an exclusive worship (Ex. 20:1–3), Jahveh is unique (Deut. 6:4): he has no consort-goddess at his side; no other god can be associated with him; none of the forces at work in the world can be termed divine, for all derive their existence from him, all are his creation. This is the fundamental creed of the Mosaic religion.[33]

---

[32] R. de Vaux, *Ancient Israel, Its Life and Institutions* (London, 1958), pp. 24-37.
[33] Here it is useful to consult the theologies of the Old Testament *e. g.* P. van Imschoot, vol. I (Paris, 1954), pp. 32–42; W. Eichrodt, *Theologie des Alten Testamentes* (Göttingen, 1957), pp. 141-6.

Two consequences of considerable importance emerge. The first is the disappearance of myths relating to sexuality; there is no longer any goddess-mother, goddess-lover, or goddess-spouse, there are no longer any divine wedding celebrations, for Jahveh cannot act either as progenitor or as lover, since he is alone in his divine order. Of all the previous sexual archetypes, the religious language of the Sinaitic religion retains only one: that of the god-Father;[34] moreover, it divests him of any correlation with a goddess-mother and so of any sexuality properly speaking. The sole archetypal relationship which remains is that between Jahveh and Israel, his people, his adopted son (Exod. 4:22–23; Deut. 1:31; cf. Osee 11:1f.; Isa. 1:2).

It goes without saying that this refinement of religious thought, unique of its kind in its Eastern environment and in complete opposition to the natural tendency of the human spirit in a totally polytheistic civilization, was not imposed on the masses in a single day nor without a struggle. Popular religion and even the official cult celebrated by the kings frequently slipped into a syncretism in which Jahveh took on the characteristics of the Canaanite Baal, whose sacred animal was the fecund bull (both a figurehead and a symbol). The image of the golden calf is evidence of this tendency (Exod. 32; 1 Kings 12:28–30). Even as late as the fifth century the unreformed Jahvism of the Elephantine Jews worshipped a divine triad in which the goddess Anath, the consort of Baal in Canaan, played the same rôle beside Jahveh.[35] But these are deviations, retrogressions, merely

---

[34] P. van Imschoot, *op. cit.,* p. 83.
[35] A. Vincent, *La religion des judéo-araméens d'Éléphantine* (Paris, 1937), pp. 622–53.

episodes in the secular struggle between the religion of Sinai and the pagan cults which tended to corrupt it.[36]

A similar phenomenon can be seen when we turn to the rites. The cultic rituals sanctioned by the Law and connected with the covenant formally prohibit practices which the contemporary cults use to hallow sexuality. For instance, a hierogamy is no longer carried out as part of the seasonal feasts, since there is no longer any divine sexual union to be imitated. Ritual prostitution, either with male or female prostitutes, is similarly proscribed and Deuteronomy imposes the death penalty for practising it (Deut. 23:18-19). With even more reason the performance of sympathetic magic, such as sexual union with animals, is forbidden on pain of the same punishment even by the very earliest codes (Exod. 22:18; Deut. 27-21; Lev. 18:23).[37]

This is not to say that in practice the Israelites, and especially those who were descendants of assimilated peoples, did not frequently revert to earlier errors: the worship of the golden calf was accompanied by orgies (Exod. 32:6) and the Book of Kings states explicitly that after the schism of Roboam, ritual prostitutes

---

[36] A certain number of critics, taking their stand on the findings of comparative religion, have postulated the existence, in pre-Babylonian Jahvism, of a mythology in which Jahveh had a consort, with whom his hierogamy was celebrated at the New Year festivities. Traces of such a mythology are said to be discernible in the Bible, in spite of corrections imposed on the texts by the Jewish priesthood at the Persian period. See G. Wildengren, "Early Hebrew Myths and their Interpretation" in *Myth, Ritual and Kingship*, pp. 176-200. In such assumptions the critics confuse the religion of Sinai, which was upheld only with difficulty at certain periods, with syncretist deviations, against which the prophets, the true upholders of tradition, rose up in protest. Cf. W. F. Albright, *From the Stone Age to Christianity*, pp. 236-40.

[37] H. Cazelles, *Études sur le Code de l'Alliance* (Paris, 1946), p. 76.

reappeared in the land (1 Kings 14:24); at the time of his reform Josias found them even in the temple at Jerusalem (2 Kings 23:7). Here yet again the discrepancy between authentic religious tradition and actual practice is evident. Tradition only triumphs after a hard struggle with the rival contemporary cults of Baal and Astarte. The legislative texts reflect a conscious and systematic reaction against these cults, which is all the stronger the clearer the threat becomes; this explains the extreme severity of Deuteronomy, which moulded the Mosaic Law to the needs of an era when it was threatened with obliteration by syncretism.[38]

This double break with environment, at the level both of the myth and of the rites, shows the determination of the religious thought of the Old Testament to abandon completely the contemporary pagan methods of establishing the sacral nature of human sexuality and of maintaining it effectively. This is not to say that sexuality and everything connected with it (fecundity, love, marriage) are no longer regarded as being sacred.

b. A New Sacral Character

On the contrary, there is every indication that the sacral character of sex continues to be recognized in Israel as it is everywhere else. All that touches upon life is sacred, because life has its source in God; an instinctive respect surrounds it, of which the prescriptions governing impurity enumerated by Leviticus are a reflection.[39] These texts have no bearing on the moral value of the action they deal with; they are simply concerned with the ritual suitability of the man and woman to approach God in the cult

[38] For this purpose of Deuteronomy, see H. Cazelles in Robert and Feuillet, *Introduction à la Bible*, vol. I (Paris, 1959), pp. 367–71.

[39] P. van Imschoot, *Théologie de l'Ancien Testament*, vol. II, pp. 204–8.

and to carry out sacred actions (Lev. 12:15). Menstrual periods and childbirth in the woman, the emission of semen in the man, the sexual union of the two, put them temporarily in an unsuitable state and necessitate certain abstentions on the part of the man (cf. 1 Kings 21:5–6; 2 Kings 11:11). We must recognize that we have here an extremely primitive and irrational conception of what is sacred and profane, of which the precise motivations may be derived from various religious ideologies: that of the fertility cult as well as that of the religion of Jahveh.

To see what meaning the sacral character of life and sex has for the Bible, we must examine the two accounts of the creation of man preserved for us in the book of Genesis. In the sphere of biblical revelation these accounts play a rôle similar to that of the creation myths in the religious literatures of Mesopotamia, Canaan, etc. Moreover, from the point of view which concerns us here, they fulfil a function similar to that otherwise fulfilled by the sexual myths.[40] Strictly speaking, however, they cannot be called myths. It is true that in order to depict the activity of God the creator in concrete terms, they employ literary devices similar to those of the myths: God "speaks", or, even better, he "fashions" the body of man, he "plants" a garden, he "forms"

---

[40] The vocabulary of this question is far from fixed. For the problem of the myth in the Old Testament, see H. Cazelles in the article "Mythe" in *Supplément au Dictionnaire de la Bible*, vol. VI, col. 246–61. J. McKenzie in *CBQ* (1959), pp. 273–4 offers a less restrictive solution: if the idea of myth is removed from the sphere of polytheistic doctrines and applied to any pictorial representation of the origin of things or of social facts, then the first chapters of Genesis fall into this category. A stricter and less equivocal definition may, however, be preferable, which makes a clear distinction between etiological accounts concerned with the origin of things and stories of gods which present us with archetypes.

the body of the woman. We must not, however, be misled
by this language studded with anthropomorphisms.[41] Its use
indicates only that it corresponds to the cultural level of a civilization which has not as yet learnt to express ideas in abstract
terms. The accounts themselves lack two of the essential elements
of the myth.

Firstly, it is not simply a story of deities with Jahveh as hero
which is being narrated: it is the story of this world, of our history
in its early stages. The highly pictorial nature of the account and
the prolific use of symbols do not affect the issue: the symbols
are intended to depict the actual state of human affairs in the
only way open to the author. Jahveh himself has no story.
His appearance is due only to the fact that he must give the initial
impetus to the only sacred history that the Bible knows: that
of the world and the humanity, in which and through whom
God's will is fulfilled. In the second place, the story of the
origins of the world and of man does not unfold in a primordial
age, an archetypal time, such as the mythologies provide for
their gods. The "beginning" in which it takes place is the beginning of cosmic and human time, the initial point of the time in
which we are at present living. If the activity of the Creator still
possesses an archetypal value, it is solely in so far as it is relevant to
the work of *homo faber,* the man who fashions, plants, and builds
and who must fit his activity into a sacred rhythm – that of the
week – which was sanctified from the very beginning by the six
days of divine work and the seventh day of rest (Gen. 2:2–3).

It is the older account of the creation (Gen. 2) which is also

[41] For the function and meaning of such anthropomorphisms, see F. Mi-
chaeli, *Dieu à l'image de l'homme* (Neuchâtel – Paris, 1950).

the more pictorial.[42] This does not mean that its author shared the unsophisticated attitude of primitive civilizations. This Jahvistic narrator, probably writing in the tenth century B. C.,[43] is a learned man sufficiently detached from the culture of his age to use its symbols discerningly and to the best advantage as vehicles for a quite amazing weight of doctrine (Gen. 2:18–25). The aspect of the human couple which he most stresses in depicting the original perfect man and woman is the mutual affection of the two partners, who have the same nature and equal dignity. It is quite clear that the woman is not on the same level as the animal: an object of possession and domination for the man (2:19–20). She is made from the man, who recognizes in her "bone that comes from his, flesh that comes from his" (2:21–23): it could not be more clearly stated that here he has "a mate of his own kind" (Gen. 2:18). He is to "cling" to her so that they become "one flesh" (2:24): the sexual union is thus to be an expression of a more profound union involving every fibre of their being. The exclamation attributed to the man on this occasion (2:23) conveys perfectly his enthusiastic and loving response to the joyful discovery of a soul-mate; his is a somewhat primitive passion in which the senses naturally play a part, but in which the essential dignity of the persons is given its full

---

[42] For details of the text the following commentaries may be usefully consulted: J. Chaine, *Le Livre de la Genèse,* series "Lectio Divina" (Paris, 1948); A. Clamer, *La Sainte Bible* (Pirot-Clamer) I, 1 (Paris, 1953); G. von Rad, *Genesis* (London, 1961). The significance of the chapters is analysed by J. de Fraine, *La Bible et l'origine de l'homme* (Bruges – Paris, 1961).

[43] H. Cazelles in Robert and Feuillet, *Introduction à la Bible,* vol. 1, p. 352; R. de Vaux, *La Genèse, Bible de Jérusalem,* p. 18; A. Clamer, *op. cit.,* pp. 38 ff.

value. It is astonishing that, in a society where polygamy was legal, the model for human marriage (cf. 2:24) should be a monogamous couple. But this ideal was the will of the Creator before sin entered the life of the couple and cast a shadow on sexuality as such: "Both went naked, Adam and his wife, and thought it no shame" (2:25).

The other account of the creation is written in a different key. Its author is generally assumed to have been a priest, probably writing in the sixth century.[44] He too assumes the same monogamy ("Man and woman both, he created them"), the same conciousness of the equal dignity of both partners ("God made man in his own image"), the same destiny of dominion over the earth, in which they are to co-operate (1:28–9). But here the most striking aspect of the couple is the fecundity to which they are jointly called ("Increase and mutiply", 1:28). It is a gift of God, the fruit of his benediction; it emanates from him and is in itself a real vocation; in it lies the whole purpose of the creation of the sexes. And, from every point of view, this divine work is "very good" (1:31). In this insistence on the primitive perfection of mankind, which the Jahvistic narrator expressed in more concrete terms by using the image of Eden where the human couple lived in innocent nakedness, the later author shows clearly that in his opinion sexuality, which is the work of God, will always be something good if the conditions of its use are in harmony with the intentions of the Creator.

In these two parallel and complementary texts we can see clearly what is the direct source of the sacral nature of marriage, of love and of fecundity. We no longer have the mythical arche-

---

[44] H. Cazelles, *op. cit.*, p. 373.

type imagined by contemporary pagan religions, but the creative word of Jahveh, the expression of his enduring will. In addition, the same divine word has imposed on human sexuality a natural curb or rule, the ideal which must be its aim. If marriage no longer has a divine archetype, it has, nonetheless, a human proto-type, created in the beginning by God, which remains a perpet-ual model and example. In it the various aspects of sexuality are no longer dissociated as was the case in pagan myths. They are united in an institution which, because it is part of God's excellent creation, sanctifies the use of sex, including in it love and fecun-dity and excluding all sexual deviations (homosexuality and bestiality). In consequence it is pointless, even bad, to try to hallow human sexuality by having recourse to magical rites such as were practised by the pagans (for instance, ritual prostitution). The sole means intended and provided by God for this purpose is marriage, in which we receive his blessing and what we now call his grace. The ideal of this society based on the family is the monogamous couple in which the two become one flesh (Gen. 2:24). In the couple the meaning of sexuality is revealed in two ways: the reciprocal personal relationship between man and wife is sealed in the flesh and their common social function is fulfilled in the reproduction of children.

The two accounts which we have just examined represent a fairly advanced intellectual stage within the biblical revelation: revelation did not begin with them. But the doctrine which they contain and put forward in opposition to pagan ideas was already implicit in the bans imposed by the Law on current cultic prac-tices in Canaan. There would be little point if the religion of Jahveh broke with the customs of the time and yet did not also reject the religious thought which inspired them. Right from the beginning the religion of Sinai involved a radical ideological change, even if this was not initially made explicit in theoretical form. It is the Jahvistic narrator and the historian-priest who take it to its logical conclusions, deeply significant ones from a theological point of view.

It is a little surprising to find such a high-minded and demanding doctrine being established in an environment which is otherwise antipathetic to abstract thought. For even Plato in the *Symposium,* where he uses the myth of the hermaphrodite (putting it, moreover, into the mocking mouth of Aristophanes), does not present the idea of the union between man and woman with more force. Yet Plato was writing some six centuries after the Jahvist historian. In addition, it is worth noticing that he is far from perceiving with the same clarity the bond which links all the different aspects of sexuality together. Nor does he show, as the first two chapters of Genesis clearly do, that the love of the human couple, their fecundity and consecration, are all strictly interdependent. In addition, he gives in the *Symposium* an important place to homosexuality in the dialectic of love and in the *Republic* makes similar allowances for warriors and permits young men considerable sexual freedom.[45] As far as marriage is concerned, he apparently accepts the social conception so well defined by Demosthenes: "We marry to beget legitimate children and to make certain that the administration of the household is in good hands."[46] The tendency towards ethical strictness

---

[45] On both these points the *Laws,* on the other hand, are emphatic in their condemnation: sexual intercourse before or outside marriage is strictly prohibited and love between young is declared to be "contrary to nature". Cf. T. Gomperz, *Les penseurs de la Grèce,* pp. 687–9.

[46] *Discourses,* 59, 122. Cf. T. Gomperz, *op. cit.,* p. 398.

evinced by the *Laws* is entirely motivated by considerations of general civic welfare and is obviously unrelated to the metaphysics of sex or the psychology of love.

It is in Genesis, therefore, that we find the ideal of the human couple most clearly expressed. Those people who today challenge this ideal do not in general do so because they do not recognize its theoretical value: who does not instinctively imagine human love in this form? But, having separated the biblical conception of the couple from its soteriological context, they despair of ever seeing it realized in practice in this world: in their opinion Genesis belongs to the realm of utopian literature. Such a view, as we shall see, bears no relation to the positive teachings of Scripture, which invariably take into account the existing material conditions of the couple's environment from both the psychological and sociological aspects. The doctrinal idealism of the first two chapters of Genesis in no way conflicts with the realism which characterizes the attitude of their inspired authors towards sexual problems. But the reconciliation of the two aspects only takes place in the eschatological perspective; thence the biblical conception of salvation must be understood.

II

THE DEVELOPMENT OF REVELATION

THE FUNDAMENTAL principles which we encountered in the two accounts of the creation of man recur constantly throughout the doctrinal development of the Old Testament. But the sacred books do not content themselves with mere repetition in various forms. There is a definite and progressive deepening of doctrine in three distinct stages. Before the prophets a certain ideal of well-ordered human sexuality is evident and at the same time we find the beginnings of reflective thought about the drama of the couple. With the prophets the comparison of the alliance between Jahveh and Israel with a marriage introduces into the subject a new element of great theological importance. Finally, in postexilic Judaism, the ideal of marriage veers noticeably in the direction of the New Testament both as regards thought and practice.

1. *The Ancient Tradition*

In the collections of ancient traditions and in the historical accounts earlier than the eighth century (according to their oral or written sources, at least) there are two types of data which call for examination. On the one hand, we find the concrete presentation of a number of couples who represent both the ideal to be followed and the actual problems which the couple encounters in life. On the other hand, we find that the drama of the couple is made the object of an examination which goes a long way towards analysing the existential situation: they were created good, yet are now burdened with the weight of sin and its consequences.

a. Some Ideal Couples

Historical writing as it was practised in Israel has little in common with what is accepted and acceptable today.[1] It differs firstly in the nature of the sources used by the authors: historical evidence is presented in forms very far removed from those we are accustomed to today. It differs too in its aim or purpose: the narrators consider the happenings in their stories purely from the viewpoint of God's will – so much so that they go far beyond the strict concerns of the historiographer and embrace those of the theologian and moralist. They are in fact masters of wisdom, who use their narratives as a channel for all sorts of teachings. Their task is made all the easier by the plastic character of the traditions they are collecting. Their doctrine is inscribed delicately in both the structure and the significant details of their writings. It is therefore of considerable interest to study the couples they choose to depict. Quite apart from the sociological facts such an inquiry

[1] A. Robert, Historique (Genre) in *Supplément au Dictionnaire de la Bible*, vol. IV, col. 7–32; Robert and Feuillet, *Introduction à la Bible*, vol. I, pp. 135–7.

will provide, an insight will be gained into their concept of the ideal couple.

Genesis is a particularly rich starting-point for such an investigation, probably because the distance of the events makes it easier to stylize the traditions which tell of them.[2] It is useful to be aware of the sociological context in which the couple Abraham and Sarah have their place. Here legal concubinage is recognized to ensure the continuance of the line (Gen. 16:1–3). To a certain extent the woman is regarded as her husband's chattel and he gives her up if the occasion demands it in order to escape the cruelties of the jealous (Gen. 20; cf. 26:1–11). The degree of kinship between half-brother and half-sister by the same father is not yet an impediment to marriage (Gen. 20:12; cf. 2 Kings 13:13; in contrast with Deut. 27:22; Lev. 20:17). The problem which is presented as vital is that of fecundity (Gen. 15:3), the sign of God's blessing: God visits Sarah (Gen. 21:1), so that she can give a son to Abraham and his promise may be fulfilled (Gen. 15:4).

The marriage of Isaac and Rebecca gives us a new and interesting sociological slant: the patriarchal family practises endogamy (Gen. 24:3–4). The over-riding concern is again that of fecundity (Gen. 24:60: the blessing upon Rebecca). Isaac's love for his wife is mentioned, but it is subsequent to and a result of the marriage (Gen. 24:67). In the case of Jacob there is once again endogamy (Gen. 28:1–2), as well as legal concubinage to ensure a more numerous offspring (Gen. 30:3–12); in addition, the patriarch has two wives equal in

---

[2] For details of the episodes quoted, reference may be made to the commentaries on Genesis recommended in note 42, p. 34.

rank (Gen. 29:15–30). The important issue for him as well as for his two wives is still that of succession, for the fecundity of a woman ensures her the love of her husband (Gen. 29:32). Nonetheless, love now takes on a certain degree of importance, the physical attraction of the woman naturally playing a part (Gen. 29:17–18): to obtain Rachel, Jacob serves Laban for seven years and "they seemed to him only a few days, because of the greatness of his love" (Gen. 29:20); when he is deceived by his cunning father-in-law, he has the courage to serve another seven years (19:30).

The story of Tamar and Juda (Gen. 38) demonstrates yet again the importance of offspring, which explains the enforcement of a law of levirate (3:8): basically Onan's offence was to refuse "to breed sons in his brother's name" (38:9–10) and Juda was no less guilty in that he neglected his duty in this respect towards his daughter-in-law (38:26); this is why, in her wild desire to obtain children, Tamar is within her rights in having recourse to the stratagem related in the story and Juda himself exculpates her (38:26).[3] It is clear that in all this the emotion of love plays little part. It is also striking that the moral code allows the man a sexual liberty *vis-à-vis* prostitutes (38:15–19) which it refuses to the married or betrothed woman (38:24): she must be burnt alive if she gives herself to a man

---

[3] It is clear that it is in complete contradiction to the original intention of the story to see Tamar as sinful. Jewish tradition lauded her conduct and considered that because of it she deserved to become the ancestor of the Messiah. It is as such that she is quoted by Matthew in his genealogy of Christ (Matt. 1:3). Cf. R. Bloch, "Juda engendra Pharès et Zara de Thamar" in *Mélanges bibliques rédigés en l'honneur d'André Robert,* pp. 381–9.

other than the one who has power over her; this detail brings out the inequality of man and woman.

The story of Joseph and the wife of his Egyptian master, who tries to seduce him, is evidence that the young Hebrew possessed a strong sense of the rights and honour of a husband and it is on this that his resolution of chastity is based (39:9). Sexual union is not permitted except in legitimate marriage; there is here a deliberate contrast with the ideas of the strange woman, who foreshadows in her conduct the seductress of Proverbs.[4] Here two conceptions of the couple clash, the one only taking the pleasure of the act into account, the other linking it with the marriage-bond in accordance with God's will.

In the later books exemplary couples are rarer. Elcana and his two wives (1 Kings 1) are another case of bigamy. Occasionally the love of the husband for one of the wives is noted, but the main concern remains that of fecundity, particularly for the wife "whom the Lord had denied motherhood" (1:5). In the marriage of David and Michol it is interesting to note that there is love between them beforehand (1 Kings 18:20-27), but the sociological context is of polygamy which permits David to marry Abigail as well as Ahinoam (1 Kings 25:43) and then to have a number of concubines (2 Kings 16:21), not to count Bethsabee, to whom we shall return presently. It is clear that the

---

[4] Cf. below p. 69. The introduction of an Egyptian woman in the rôle of seductress does not mean the writer intends to discredit all Egyptian women. In Egyptian wisdom literature too there are warnings against seductresses: Wisdom of Ani, III, 13 (cf. Pritchard, *Ancient Near Eastern Texts,* p. 420); S. Schott, *Les chants d'amour de l'Egypte ancienne,* translated from the German (Paris, 1956), p. 51.

THE DEVELOPMENT OF REVELATION

man, and especially the king, is of far greater importance than the woman in any marriage.

Psalm 45, an ancient royal epithalamion,[5] does, however, give an honourable place to the bride. Although here the joyousness of the wedding is seen from the outside by a spectator and not by the participants, we find not only the concern of fecundity clearly stated (17) but also, less directly, that of the attachment between bride and bridegroom (11–12). From the sociological point of view it is interesting to note that the bride is a Phoenician princess (13), a stranger who must therefore "forget her own nation and the house of her father" (Ps. 45:11; cf. Gen. 2:24) and doubtless the gods of her country too, if she is to obtain the blessing of the God of Israel.

Such an investigation is instructive. In the first place it clarifies for us the hierarchy of values prevalent at the time. Procreation is essential because it ensures the continuation of the race. Human affection between the marriage partners, although it makes an occasional discreet appearance, in general takes up a very subordinate position: physical love, which has a direct bearing on fecundity, takes precedence over the emotion, which is less useful in this respect. In any case there is little question of marriage "for happiness", even if God in fact gives the partners happiness in abundance. From this point of view, the conception of marriage and love is very far removed from our modern romanticism in which the picture of heavenly joys within the grasp is allowed to transfigure the real nature of marriage. The wise men of the Bible, like the people they

---

[5] E. Podechard, *Le Psautier,* Traduction littérale et explication historique, vol. I (Lyon, 1949), pp. 196–203; H. Kraus, *Psalmen,* Biblischer Kommentar Altes Testament (Neukirchen, 1956), pp. 330–8.

depict, are far more objective. To them the word "couple" does not suggest the solitude of lovers who are indifferent to the world which surrounds them. On the contrary, the couple is a part of social life and has a function to fulfil in it. Here we see the connection with Genesis 1–2. Nonetheless, the sociological evidence afforded by the books from the twelfth chapter of Genesis to the second book of Kings indicates, even by itself, the discrepancy existing between the ideal put forward by the accounts of the creation, and still aspired to by mankind, and human reality even as we see it from the best of the examples. This lucidity of approach is even more in evidence when the writers depict the tragedy of couples whose love turns to corruption.

b. The Tragic Aspects of the Couple

Here, too, the most profound thinking is to be found in the chapters with which the "Jahvist" sacred history begins.[6] Immediately after presenting the prototype couple in their original perfection, the writer shows them being plunged straight into tragedy (Gen. 3). It is true that in his capacity as an historian it is the emergence of sin as an historical fact that he wishes to record in this page of subtly scaled psychological observations. But this original sin, the prologue of the whole drama of humanity and the starting-point of the plan of salvation which God brings

[6] In addition to the commentaries on Genesis referred to above, mention may be made of the analyses of A.-M. Dubarle, *Le péché originel dans l'Écriture,* series "Lectio Divina" (Paris, 1958), pp. 39–74; L. Ligier, *Péché d'Adam et péché du monde,* I, L'Ancien Testament, series "Théologie" (Paris, 1960), pp. 171–286; G. Lambert, "Le drame du jardin d'Eden" in *Nouvelle Revue Théologique,* 1954, pp. 917–48 and 1044–72.

46

about with the passing of the ages, is not the sin of an abstract man who offends the Creator in the solitude of his individual conscience. It is not even simply the sin of Adam, the first head of the human race and a "type of the Adam who was to come" (Rom. 5:12–19). It is the shared sin of the prototype couple;[7] for Man does not exist except as man and woman. We must therefore examine closely what the man-woman relationship becomes in the commission of the sin and in the consequences of their act. By reading between the lines of the account in this way we are far from investing the author with didactic intentions foreign to his purpose. He belongs to the same school of learned men who have handed down to us the story of the reign of David,[8] in which there are several tragic couples to whom we shall refer again later – David and Bethsabee, Amnon and Tamar – and it is not surprising, therefore, that he sees in Adam and Eve the first of them, their prototype in fact.

The behaviour of the partners in committing the first sin is of great significance and we cannot here entirely neglect some discussion of the nature of that sin itself. Certain exegetes have thought they were right to see sexual characteristics in the symbols and expressions used to describe the sin.[9] They regard the serpent as a parallel of fertility cults; the eating of the

[7] As is emphasized by L. Ligier, *op. cit.,* pp. 219–31.

[8] J. Delorme in Robert and Feuillet, *Introduction à la Bible,* vol. I, pp. 418–20. Ligier is not wrong in examining parallels which suggest that Gen. 3 is a "royal parable" (*op. cit.,* pp. 232–86). But the point of view from which we are approaching the subject here necessarily orientates our analysis differently.

[9] J. Coppens, *La connaissance du bien et du mal et le péché du Paradis* (Louvain – Bruges – Paris, 1948), assembles all the evidence which can be interpreted in this way.

forbidden fruit they regard as a magic act intended to awaken sexuality; the use of sex, obtained without the consent of God, is symbolized by the knowledge of good and evil, as is shown by the awakening of shame and the sense of sexual modesty (Gen. 3:7). Such research into the possible background of the symbols is not without interest, but it should not be allowed to obscure the links between this account and wisdom literature. This prototype sin is, in fact, the transgression of an order – or rather of a prohibition – given by God, exactly as is any transgression of the commandments. The divine will is here presented in the form of an alimentary prohibition, but this is only a metaphorical expression and its deeper meaning is undeniable. In fact the object of the temptation is not so much that the fruit is good to eat, pleasant to look at, and gives desirable knowledge (Gen. 3:6), but the desire to be like gods (3:5). In this connotation the knowledge of good and evil is to be understood either as universal knowledge or as an usurped dominion over moral good and evil which reverses the divine order of things (cf. Isa. 5:20–21) instead of being subject to it with an upright conscience (cf. Amos 5:14–15; Isa. 7:15). Finally, behind the serpent ("of all the beasts which the Lord had made, none could match the serpent in cunning" Gen. 3:1), it is easy to see the form of the archetypal Serpent, God's chief adversary, "the monstrous serpent . . . the great beast of the sea" (Isa. 27:1): it is not without significance that the Old Testament uses elsewhere this ancient mythical symbol to represent the forces of chaos which are from the beginning in conflict with God the creator and which he has to conquer in order to accomplish his work (cf. Isa. 51:9; Ps. 74:13–14; 89:10–11). In short, the sin of the first couple is essentially an act of the "heart" (in the

48

biblical sense of the word) and it seems unlikely that the sacred writer intends its concrete translation into an usurped use of sexuality which has been acquired by an act of magic.

Nonetheless, it is obvious that the man-woman relationship is involved in the act and that it is this which causes its corruption. The woman was given to the man as "a mate of his own kind" (Gen. 2:18); but she turns seductress to lead him astray into evil. The man was given to the woman as her head, her leader, created before her; but, yielding to her seduction, he follows her in the path which she has chosen on her own initiative. So instead of a communion in the unity of one flesh (2:24) and a common submission to their condition as creatures (cf. 3:1), there is no longer anything between them but complicity in a Promethean undertaking which alienates them from the Creator.

One is, of course, at liberty to speculate on these facts: the acquisition of this usurped "knowledge" possibly implies the consummation of the sexual act in which the man and woman "know" one another in their human nature. They should "know" one another in their condition as created beings, yet they imagine that they will "know" one another like gods . . . It is not difficult for theological thought to develop in this way the positive facts given us by the biblical account. The latter evokes the prototype sin, through which sin itself makes its appearance in the world (Rom. 5:12), by using symbols which veil its concrete reality. Nonetheless, this reality is not completely hidden. In part, at least, it is linked with the awakening of self-consciousness, which is the divinely-ordained test of whether man can accept himself as he is. Man, however, refuses to acknowledge that he is a creature, in the hope of transcending his state: "As soon as you eat this fruit your eyes will be opened and you yourselves will be like gods." This "man" who sins is, in fact, "man and woman"; and can one make a distinction, in the case of the two partners in such a relationship, between dawning of consciousness of self and experience or awareness of the other? To see the problem of original sin from this point of view is not to exclude its having some sexual component. Yet such a theological development, however legitimate, goes far beyond the explicit data we gain from Genesis.

However that may be, the mutual love of the man and the woman is vitiated at its roots by their common commission of sin; and the consequences of their sin rebound on their love. No sooner have they eaten the fruit than "the eyes of both were opened, and they became aware of their nakedness" (3:7). The irony of the situation is obvious: in place of the transcendental knowledge that they both hoped for, they have nothing but the realization of their own miserable nature. The illusory dream of becoming like gods gives place to a cruel awareness of their sinful condition. The mention of their nakedness at this point in the story is in intentional contrast with the earlier reference just after the creation of the couple: "Both went naked, Adam and his wife, and thought it no shame" (2:25). It is, therefore, on this very point that a change has taken place. The feeling of shame which is from now on bound up with sexuality is a token of lost innocence, of the wound inflicted on the power of loving, of the disorder introduced by the inflaming of the passions, of the shadow which has fallen between the two partners.

The end of the scene effectively underlines the state of psychological separation in which the sinning couple find themselves. Made in order to live in the most intimate unity, they tried to find fulfilment in an act which would have put them beyond the Divine Law. But now the two conspirators are forced back upon themselves and for the first time know loneliness: they are no longer truly at one, for Adam throws the blame on Eve (3:12), while Eve tries to put the responsibility for it all on the serpent who beguiled her (3:13). Finally we have God's sentence, which sets out the permanent consequences of the sin for the couple who have committed it and for all the couples who are to come after them in their lineage. The man-woman relationship, instead of ensuring the couple's profound unity in an atmosphere of mutual love, will be characterized by the man's domination of the woman and the passionate attachment of the woman to her husband (3:16). The rôle of head granted to the man is thus degraded to the power of enslavement; the woman's love, formerly that of a companion "of his own kind", is degraded to a covetous desire. As for fecundity, the normal outcome of sexual intercourse, it will from henceforth only take place in a context of suffering (3:16). Here we are presented with a picture of the present condition of the human couple: created good, they remain impaired by sin and are in need of redemption.

It is clear that it is a carefully-balanced conception of sexuality which the biblical writer gives his readers. By juxtaposing the account of the creation (Gen. 2) and that of the original sin (Gen. 2), he excludes both a dualistic conception which would justify its view of sexuality as an evil by pointing to the concomitant disorder and suffering and a conception with no basis in reality which would deny the disorder and encourage hopes of a facile liberation from suffering.[10] Something does, however,

[10] The romantic conception of the couple oscillates between these two

remain of the state of things created by God in the first paradise: an institution which, as such, remains good, in which love and the use of sex remain good, and of which the natural outcome, fecundity, remains a blessing. But the paradise on earth, the vision which haunts the dreams of every couple, remains an unattainable realm: Adam and Eve have been banished from Eden (3:23). The theological description of the state of man after original sin is equally and precisely applicable to the sexuality and life of the couple: *vulneratus in naturalibus*. At the personal level the human individual has lost the unity of his nature; he experiences an inner tension between his anarchic faculties, and especially between the flesh and the spirit, in the words of St. Paul (Gal. 5:17; Rom. 7:14ff.).[11] At the social level the human community has lost its natural unity, and in its place there has arisen a dialectical relationship between nations, cultures and classes. The result has been the same for the couple whose living union was designed to reproduce the image of God: their union has been shattered and God's image defaced.

extremes. On the one hand the love of Tristan and Iseult is an evil fate which hangs over their destiny and leads to their death. On the other hand, the popular literature of all ages is made up of fabulous stories in which handsome princes marry simple shepherdesses and "live happily ever after".

[11] It is important not to interpret St. Paul's language according to the categories of Greek thought, for which body and spirit constitute two parts of the human whole. The flaw in nature is not only of a moral order. It has its roots in the physical conditioning of our spiritual activity and is particularly in evidence in the sexual sphere, since this latter is closely linked with the nervous system. From this point of view psychoanalytical investigation of the instincts, which reveals many traumatisms and neuroses of the unbalanced mind, touches upon what theology calls the "flaw" in human nature.

c. The Tragic Aspects of the Couple in the History of Man

It is not difficult to corroborate this analysis of the third chapter of Genesis by gathering together, from the biblical accounts from Genesis to the book of Kings, the details which show the permanent tragedy of the human couple's situation. Even in those households which approach the ideal desired by God, infecundity, the supposed mark of the divine displeasure, can be a source of shame and grief: it is such for Abraham (Gen. 15:3) and for Anna, the mother of Samuel (1 Kings 1:2–11). It is true that the monogamy of the first couple is not indeed preserved as the rule for marriage – doubtless custom authorizes departures sanctioned by the law of Moses – but it is significant that Genesis shows polygamy starting in Cain's family and that Lamech, its initiator, is a bloodthirsty man who also initiates the idea of a ruthless vendetta (Gen. 4:19–24). Experience shows that it is a source of disagreement and rivalry (Anna and Phenenna, 1 Kings 1:4–6), even when it is simply a case of legal concubinage (Sarai and Agar, Gen. 16:3–6); in the case of the kings, the multiplication of wives can cause more serious disorders (Solomon, 1 Kings 11:1–4) and it is against these that Deuteronomy issues his warning (17:17).

Marriage for love, however, can lead to disagreements between a young and inexperienced man and his more realistic parents (Samson, Judges 14:1–4) and runs the risk of ending in cruel disappointment and a swift separation (Judges 14:12–20). Even more so does the satisfaction of lust with prostitutes (Judges 16, 1–3) and the unbridled passion by which a man is enslaved and loses something of his manliness (Samson and Dalila, Judges 16:4–21). When such a passion takes hold of a man

53

it can lead him to acts of violence for which reparation must later be made (Exod. 22:16–17; Deut. 22:23–9): this is what happens in the story of Dina (Gen. 34) and of the wife of the Levite of Gibea (Judges 19:11–30). The tragic story of Amnon, the son of David, violating his half-sister Tamar before being assassinated by Absalom, the uterine brother of Tamar (2 Kings 13:1–38), gives rise to one of the rare searching psychological analyses offered by the Old Testament: the desire and the cunning of the enamoured young man, the brutal satisfaction of his lust, which then immediately undergoes a revulsion and changes to disgust (2 Kings 13:1–20).

We are presented, too, with adulterous love, of which the classic example is David and Bethsabee: the king's passion brings about the death of Urias and later the death of the illegitimate child and is the beginning of all the domestic tragedies which are to darken the final years of his reign (2 Kings 11–12). It is true that the sociological context of the time admits finally of an honourable solution to the problem: David takes Bethsabee into his harem and she gives birth to Solomon who will be heir to the throne. Even a legitimate wife can, however, be a source of sin and we are given a significant example of this in the couple, Achab and Jezabel (3 Kings 16:31): the foreign wife induces her husband to worship other gods and to perpetrate crimes and injustices (Story of Naboth's vineyard, 3 Kings 21). Finally there are the sexual perversions which are derided or denounced by the biblical writers: the carnal relationship of Lot and his daughters (Gen. 19:31–8), the vice of Sodom which calls down the anger of heaven (Gen. 18–19), ritual prostitution which leads to idolatry by way of debauchery (Num. 25:1–18). All these facts show what is the real situation of sexuality and the human

54

couple in a sinful world: a frail thing, constantly threatened and far removed from its original ideal.

d. Towards the Redemption of the Couple

Yet surely the situation is not one of total despair. Surely God, who has inaugurated a plan of salvation for the world, intends to rescue the human couple from their misery too. At the stage of revelation that concerns us here, the indications pointing in this direction are as yet slight, but they do exist. For in this world's struggle between the woman and the Serpent, God has arrayed himself on the side of the Woman and her seed and has promised her that she will finally crush the head of the serpent (Gen. 3:15). In fact, the couple have not been deprived because of their sin of the blessing given to them in the beginning and evinced outwardly by their fecundity (Gen. 1:28): according to the Jahvist narrator, Eve says of her first son: "I have been enriched by the Lord with a man-child" (Gen. 4:1) and according to the historian-priest, the birth of Seth is the fulfilment of the blessing given to Adam by the Creator in the beginning (Gen. 5:1-3). Later even the outbreak of crimes which provoke the type-punishment of the flood (Gen. 6:5-12) in no way changes God's fundamental intention; and at the time of his covenant with Noe, God explicitly renews the commandment given in the beginning: "Increase and multiply, and fill the earth" (Gen. 9:1; cf. 1:28).[12]

---

[12] The text of the nuptial blessing in the marriage liturgy emphasizes this aspect of the biblical account: "God, who joinest woman to man, and hast endowed this primal fellowship of theirs with the one and only blessing that was not forfeited either in punishment of the first sin or

It is then evident that the attitude of the people of Israel towards sexuality is an undeniable advance on that of the surrounding pagan communities. The revelation of the one God has put an end to erroneous attempts at sacralization. At the same time a strict Law, while tolerating *ad duritiam cordis* (Matt. 19:8) practical measures which are far from conforming to the primordial ideal (polygamy, concubinage, divorce), forces a return to an order of things in which deviations most in conflict with the natural law are proscribed (bestiality, homosexuality, the woman's adultery or the man's with a married woman) and which respects the demands of religion in demanding faithful adherence. Considering the limitations imposed by the customs of the time, following so many centuries of ignorance and sin, this is clearly a first step towards the final restoration to come. If the institution of marriage has not yet been accorded its full rights, if redeeming grace is not yet explicitly promised to men for the sanctification of their conjugal love, nonetheless the rule of sexual morality imposed on the people of God is already a means of canalizing anarchic lust and thus to a certain extent ensuring the characteristics which Christian doctrine will demand of marriage: *bonum prolis* and, to a lesser extent, *bonum fidei* and *bonum sacramenti* (that is, faithfulness and perpetuity). New advances in this respect are made in the next two stages of Old Testament history.

---

under sentence of the flood . . ." The formulation of this prayer should perhaps be reconsidered in view of the critical problems posed by Gen. 1–11. Its content, however, stresses an indispensable element of the theology of marriage.

2. The Teaching of the Prophets

a. The Marriage Theme

The primitive conception of marriage in Israel excluded any hallowing of the couple, of sexuality and of the institution of marriage itself by reference to a divine archetype of a mythical nature. It is precisely on this point that the preaching of the prophets introduces innovations into religious thought in the form of a new kind of archetype quite unknown to paganism. It is no longer an archetype which has to be sought in a story of gods taking place at some primordial time. It is to be found at the heart of the sacred history which is unfolding here on earth and which gives its profound meaning to Israel's experiences. This archetype is the covenant granted by God to his people.[13]

Every marriage is a contract *(berith)* between a man and a woman (cf. Mal. 2:14; Prov. 2:17). The legal relationship which results is closely connected with affective elements: love, fidelity, troth *(chesed*[14]*)*. In the same way the covenant *(berith)* made on Sinai, while in essence a contract, goes far beyond the merely legal requirements: on God's side it presupposes love, fidelity, *chesed* (Exod. 34:6–7; Deut. 7:7–8); on Israel's side it also demands love, fidelity, *chesed* (Deut. 6:4; Osee 4:1; 6:6). To gain a clear and accurate picture of the relationship between God and his people, as it is laid down by the covenant on Sinai, it is not sufficient to compare it to the treaties between lord and vassal,

---

[13] A. Neher, *L'essence du prophétisme* (Paris, 1955), pp. 247–57.
[14] On the idea of *chesed,* which it is difficult to render in one word, see J. Guillet, *Thèmes bibliques* (Paris, 1951), pp. 43–6; A. Neher, *op. cit.,* pp. 254–69; C. Spicq, *Dieu et l'homme dans le Nouveau Testament,* series "Lectio Divina" (Paris, 1961), p. 17 gives a bibliography of the subject.

which provide the legal model for the contract. It is essential to bear in mind too the comparison with the relationship established between a man and woman at the time of their marriage. The concept of the covenant is thus considerably enriched by the affective overtones it acquires: Israel and her God are bound by ties of the heart and not only by those of law. There is yet another consequence of far-reaching importance: the relationship between God and Israel becomes the model and example for the man-woman relationship in marriage, in other words it becomes the sacred archetype of the human couple. It is true that the fecundity of the couple receives less emphasis in this archetype than the question of the personal relationship between the husband and wife. But having personified the people of God with feminine traits, the prophets sustain the image logically and present the Israelites as the sons of Jahveh's Spouse.

This parallel between human marriage and the covenant between Jahveh and his people is developed at length by the prophets. Far from turning into abstract thought the love which introduces a dramatic element into the experience of the man-woman relationship, it uses it to evoke in a concrete way certain mysterious aspects of the drama of Israel. Human love, impaired by sin, can actually be damaged by tragic incidents: a wanton wife's infidelity, the scorned husband's wrath, repudiation or putting to death of the unfaithful wife. Israel's relationship with its God provides a parallel. Israel bears its share of human sin, which draws it into infidelities that assume a real rejection of the Mosaic Covenant. The unfaithful wife thus inevitably draws down upon herself the wrath of her husband and has to submit to the penalties written into the contract (cf. Exod. 23:21; Lev. 26:14–35; Deut. 28:15–68). It is in the light of the human tragedy enacted in the lives of so many couples that the spiritual tragedy of the sinning Israel, its situation before God, the fate which awaits it in history, all become intelligible.

Nonetheless, there is a difference. In this spiritual tragedy it is no longer a man who plays the part of the husband, but the living God. It is this which completely alters the perspective of the final outcome. For God's love, his fidelity, his *chesed* are absolute and immutable values. Whatever the conduct of his chosen people, God cannot go back on his eternal plan which he started to unveil when he made a covenant with his people. His anger against sin cannot obliterate his faithfulness to his promises and his contract. His fidelity, in fact, is a creative one which desires the return and conversion of the sinful people in order to restore the relationship of the covenant in its ideal purity. God's love continues even while he chastises. It is a magnanimous love ever ready to pardon, more powerful than the sins of men; its chief desire is to be united again with them in a new covenant which would not suffer the same fate as the first. At the level of the divine archetype for marriage, we have to envisage something for which there was no provision in Israel's law where it concerned adulterous women (Deut. 24:1–4; Jer. 3:1) and of which current practice gives us very little experience: complete renunciation of righteous anger, re-acceptance of the pardoned wife, a new *berith* more perfect than the first: "Everlastingly I will betroth thee to myself, favour and redress and mercy of mine thy dowry; by the keeping of his troth thou shalt learn to know the Lord" (Osee 2:21–2). This is the final intention of the divine betrothals; and their aim, foreseen from the first covenant, thwarted by human sin, will finally be accomplished in a redemption which will manifest the love of the divine Spouse in its fullness.

b. Development of the Theme

The confrontation of the tragedy as enacted by the human couple and the tragedy as enacted by the people of God is found in many prophetic texts. It originates with Osee. The starting-point is not simply a meditation on the meaning of love and its paradoxical power; it is a personal experience, analogous in certain aspects to the symbolic actions of the prophets, but here including all the affectivity of the divine messenger. It is true that the two accounts left by the prophet (Osee 1 and 3) are difficult to reconcile and the sequence of events hard to follow. In the first account the Lord's inspiration directs Osee to wed a wanton woman and breed wantons (1:2); this is an image of what Israel is for Jahveh: a wanton spouse whose children have been defiled by the practice of idolatry. In the second account Osee receives the command to love the "wife that will have gallants a-courting her" (3:1) and so he buys her back and enforces a purifying abstinence on her; here, too, we have a symbol of what God desires to do for his sinful people. Are there here two parallel recensions of the same symbolic marriage[15] or two significant acts which evoke in turn the corruption of the faithless Israel, then the redemptive love of God?[16] To decide with any certainty is difficult. The essential is anyway not on this level, but on that of the archetypal marriage of which Osee reveals the vicissitudes:

[15] Cf. A. Gelin in Robert and Feuillet, *Introduction à la Bible,* vol. I, pp. 494–6.

[16] This is J. Steinmann's position, see *Le prophétisme biblique des origines à Osée,* series "Lectio Divina," pp. 189–92. Gomer's prostitution is to be understood in a figurative sense (Osee 1): the prophet's first marriage is honourable socially. The woman in chap. 3 is no longer Gomer, but a second woman, redeemed and married symbolically. Any other interpretation of the story is described as "fictional" (p. 192).

the marriage of Jahveh and Israel.[17] The prophet draws on human experience to invest God with the psychology of a husband who loves, who suffers when his love is scorned, who pardons and reconstructs the home that has been ruined. What husband would act in this way? But this is how God acts towards men; more than any human husband he has loved and suffered, yet he wants to pardon all who return to him, he will purify them and resume the relationship of love with them. The improbability that this situation should arise in a social environment which punishes a woman's adultery so harshly, throws into relief the grandeur of the revelation uttered by the prophet: the parable of the prodigal son and the forgiving father (Luke 15) is scarcely more telling in this respect than the story of the husband who takes back his wanton wife.

This revelation is set out plainly in the chapter which expands the symbol at length (Osee 2).[18] Here the relationship between God and Israel is developed by way of using the characteristics of the couple in the drama. The question of fecundity has only a fleeting mention: the Israelites are the children of the woman whom Jahveh has taken for his wife (2:4). The essential is the problem of love. Human psychology here enables the prophet to illuminate the mystery of the relationship between God and men by reference to the personal relationship of husband and

[17] From this point of view, the symbolic acts of chapters 1 and 3 do not have the same significance: the first is a parallel of the Mosaic covenant, in which Jahveh binds himself to a "wanton"; the second represents the redemption and the new covenant.

[18] J. Steinmann breaks up chap. 2 into eight short prophecies with different historical contexts. It is possible to make a case for this. But it is surely better to respect the unity of the very elaborate whole, since this is what the editor of the book of Osee intended.

61

wife. He notes, for instance, the jealous love of God who received no gratitude for his gifts (2:10) and whom the wife scorned by her adultery and prostitution (2:4, 7); the betrayed love which repudiates (2:4) and punishes with severity (2:5–6; 11–15) in order to bring about self-scrutiny and repentance (2:9, 13); the persevering love which despite all disappointments and setbacks is still willing to woo (2:16), to obtain once again a loving response as in former times (2:17); the love which will finally triumph since, having purified the guilty wife, it will renew the conjugal bond in a paradisal perfection (2:20). It is important to notice this end of the tragedy. It actually links the perfect realization of the marriage archetype between God and his people with the new covenant, which will only come in the course of time. We should perhaps risk a neologism here and speak of a teleotype rather than an archetype and this demonstrates how profoundly the religious symbolism to which the biblical revelation has recourse differs from those symbolisms employed by the oriental myths. The latter projected the data of a universal and immutable human experience into the absolute of a "primordial time". The Bible transforms these same data in the very moment of using them, for it re-interprets them in the light of an historical experience, made up of extraordinary events, which takes its starting-point from the covenant on Sinai and has as its objective an eschatological covenant.

By introducing the theme of marriage into the expression of doctrine, Osee has said everything that is essential. After him and dependent upon him, other prophets take it up. But as it is never linked to the same extent with their experience as men, they do not achieve the same existential profundity. For them it is a literary theme, developed more systematically at certain points, but one that has become a commonplace of theological language. The first example is provided by Isaias. It is no more than an indirect allusion in the love-song of Isaias 5:1–7: the allegory of the vine probably hides a conjugal symbol, the vine being a metaphor for the fruitful wife (cf. Ps. 128:4). The only aspect of the tragedy which they emphasize is that of unselfish, unappreciated and jealous love which eventually turns to anger. No prospect of redemption is suggested by this parable of the divine judgment.

The interweaving of the two symbols of the vine and the woman is found again in Jeremias (2:20:25) where it is used to stigmatize the infidelity of Israel. In addition, the same prophet develops certain aspects of the imagery: the innocence of the desert betrothal in affection *(chesed)* and love (2:2) is evoked dolefully by "the loved friend of thy girlhood's days" who is also the "father" of the woman (3:4); depicted also is his horror at the woman's corruption: having prostituted herself with innumerable lovers, she has the boldness to lay claim still to the title of spouse, in conflict with the stipulation of the Law (3:1–5; Deut. 24:1–4). There is also the parallel of the two wanton sisters, Israel and Juda: the first has been repudiated according to the Law and nonetheless the second falls into worse sin, yet Jahveh in his mercy invites her again to return to him (Jer. 3:6–13). Finally he notes the perseverance of divine love which will in the end bring back to him the Virgin of Israel: then the wife will come back to her husband (31:21–2) and the joy of regained love will recall that of the first betrothal (31:2–6).

This eschatological slant with which the message of Jeremias ends transposes on to the plane of conjugal symbolism what is elsewhere applied to the new covenant (31:31–4). The prophet lets it be clearly understood that there will be no question of a natural conclusion to the story, but rather of a miracle of divine grace, capable of overcoming the hardness of the human heart and transforming its infidelity into love. Here the symbolism of the marriage again cuts across that of God as the Father who saves his children (31:7–9, 18–20) and the Shepherd who leads his sheep towards good pastures (31:10–4). This shows that God's relationship with men cannot be defined by reference to any one aspect of human experience; but to represent the covenant itself, the image of the couple is to some extent indispensable.

Ezechiel, too, takes up this image in two long allegories. The first (Ezech. 16) uses it as the means of integrating the whole history of Israel in the guise of a drama of love. The archetypes of Jahveh the Father and Jahveh the Spouse are combined, since Israel is a foundling, saved from death by the Lord out of pity, brought up and finally espoused when "ripe for love" (16:1–8). The psychology of the love of the man, considerate and delicate, desirous of protecting the woman and overwhelming her with presents (16:8–14), underlines by contrast the shamefulness of the woman's infidelity, inspired by her pride, of her offering herself to all comers, giving away her husband's presents to casual lovers, finally even sacrificing her legitimate children (16:15–29). The adulterous wife has behaved in a manner far worse than the worst prostitutes (16:30–4); she has outdone in her dishonourable conduct her mother (a pagan nation), her elder sister (Samaria) and her younger sister (Sodom) (16:44–52). She, too, is to undergo the legal punishment of adulterous women (Deut. 22:22; Lev. 20:10); but as cruel irony will have it, it is her lovers (the foreign peoples) who will carry it out (Ezech. 16:35–43). The historical allusions to the political alliances of Jerusalem and the national catastrophe that they are about to provoke are here a gloss and control the development of the allegory. But the final outlook is of a free pardon, a restoration which will encompass even the sister-nations (Samaria and Sodom, 16:53–8) a new covenant which will remake the unity of mankind and endure for ever (16:59:63): the sister-nations (Samaria and Sodom, representing the non-Jewish world[19]) will become daughter-nations of the new Jerusalem, the spouse of God (16:61).

Ezechiel's second allegory, which makes use of a sociological fact of the time (bigamy), is linked with the earlier theme only at one particular point: the parallel infidelity and punishment of the two sisters, the unfaithful wives of the Lord, Samaria and Jerusalem (cf. Jer. 3:6–11); the jealousy of an unrequited love which turns to anger is the only subject to be developed, since eschatological promises are not dealt with here.

By way of contrast it is this last point which provides the essential theme of the Second Isaias.[20] The divorce merited by the wife's infidelity is spoken of only in the past (54:6–8) and "the wife of

---

[19] To be precise: the non-Judaic world. The return of Samaria, now a daughter-nation of Jerusalem, clearly represents the restoration of the unity of Israel, broken at the time of the schism. Sodom, on the other hand, is referred to as the typical pagan nation, where all the vices of paganism flourished with particular strength. In addition, paganism is represented by other towns: Nineveh in the book of Jonas; Babylon, Tyre, etc. in Psalm 87:4. It is symptomatic that in Ezechiel the bride of Jahveh is no longer the people of Israel, but the city of Jerusalem which, as the capital, personifies Israel as a whole. The use of feminine traits to evoke a city is a familiar feature of Old Testament poetry. The image of a city as wife and mother is thus perfectly in keeping.

[20] On the date of the Second Isaias cf. A. Gelin in Robert and Feuillet, *Introduction à la Bible,* vol. I, pp. 550–1; J. Steinmann, *Le livre de la consolation d'Israël,* series "Lectio Divina" (Paris, 1960), pp. 85 ff.

his youth, long cast away" is recalled by the Lord and he promises that "love that takes pity on thee shall be eternal" (54:6, 8). Here it is the final success of love that is evoked by the betrothal theme. And the eschatological Jerusalem, bought back and espoused by her Creator (54:5), who will grant her his covenant of peace (54:10), is no longer the sinful city which merited God's wrath. It is a transformed Jerusalem, a continuation of the old which yet escapes the historic condition of fallen humanity: a trans-historical Jerusalem, one might say. Between God and this Jerusalem the mystery of a perfect marriage will be realized and this will give a concrete existence to the archetype of the couple: the permanent love of the husband (54:10); the wife's forgetting of the time of desolation and seeming abandonment when her situation was that of the unfaithful wife (54:4–6); a miraculous fecundity far greater than her previous fecundity which was limited by her condition of being a particular nation (54:1–3). The ideal spouse of Jahveh is no longer the historical people of Israel but redeemed humanity as a whole. The marriage-contract of Sinai did no more than foreshadow on the figurative plane of the Old Testament what will be accomplished in all its fullness in the time to come.

The teaching in Isaias 60-2 is similar.[21] Blending together several literary themes, the author presents once again the fecundity of the new Jerusalem (60:4) whose joy is that of the bride adorned with her husband's gifts, whose glory that of the bride once again a pure virgin who gives all for her husband's happiness (62:4–5). The profound transformation of the city-spouse, the feminine personification of humanity as it faces

[21] On the Third Isaias, cf. A. Gelin, *op. cit.*, pp. 567–9.

God, is worth emphasizing. From the prostitute that she was (Isa. 1:21), she has become both virgin (Isa. 62:5) and mother of many children. This return to original innocence after God's triumph over sin is a miracle of grace and it is this which is at the heart of the prophetical promises.

c. Doctrinal Significance of the Prophetical Texts

The prophetical texts therefore spring from the human experience of the couple, seen in its various aspects (marriage, love, fecundity), and are intended to evoke the supernatural reality which is its archetype: the covenant between God and men. This reality is evoked in two stages. Firstly, the imperfect stage of the Mosaic covenant. At this stage the experience of love as far as humanity (the wife) is concerned resembles that of human love as it actually is: impaired and subject to the set-backs and failures of adultery and prostitution. Next comes the perfect stage of the eschatological covenant, in which the experience of love will regain the characteristics of a human love only dreamed of at present, shielded from the bondage of evil, rejoining a paradisical prototype impossible to attain without the help of redeeming grace.

This evocation, religious in essence, throws light retrospectively on the human reality which is its point of departure. It is of real importance to notice that the picture it paints of love is an ideal picture which depicts the couple as they should be, in harmony with the design of the Creator, after redeeming grace has triumphed over sin. In this eschatological perspective, and in it alone, human love, lived in the sacrament of marriage which effectively sanctifies sexuality, will regain its characteristic marks: union in love, fecundity, indissoluble

67

perpetuity (*fides, proles, sacramentum*, in the words of St. Augustine). Such is therefore the ideal towards which the couple must aspire if they want to model themselves not only on their original prototype, but on their divine archetype too. They are able to do so from the moment when they participate in the redemptive grace which is to restore sinful humanity to its original paradisical state. The Christian theology of marriage is by no means as yet completely explained by such a presentation since the prophets do not draw all the conclusions which we have just been discussing; nonetheless it is possible to say that it already underlies their teaching.

3. The Ideal of Marriage in Postexilic Judaism

Between the captivity of Babylon and the New Testament there is an era when the promise of the new covenant already belongs to the past. The Jewish people are waiting for its actual realization; nonetheless, their way of life and institutions, although both have developed with time, are still bound up with the Mosaic covenant. From the point of view which concerns us here, the juridical rules of conduct handed down by tradition still flourish with all the imperfections which we noticed (notably, the possibility of polygamy and divorce). Nonetheless, it is certain that the ideal of marriage has been refined and, to a certain extent, practice has fallen into line with it. There are many relevant texts here and we must be content with a brief survey. Most of them give rules of conduct for life, either legal or moral, in the form of prophetic exhortations or sapiential teaching. Only one, which is not didactic but lyric, has as its subject the personal relationship of the couple: this is the Song of Songs which, for this reason, merits special consideration.

a. Prophetical and Sapiential Texts

Malachias 2:14–16 represents an important advance in the biblical conception of marriage. The prophet recounts one of God's grievances against his people. Why is' God dissatisfied, why does he turn away from Israel's offerings? "Because the Lord bears witness to her wrongs, that wife of thy manhood's age, whom now thou spurnest, thy partner, thy covenanted bride. . . . Spurn her not, the wife of thy manhood's age." This prophetic diatribe entails a demand for affection and fidelity, which even goes as far as the indissolubility of the matrimonial *berith* and far beyond the tolerances of the Torah.[22] To support this demand, the prophet seems to appeal, in the rather obscure verse quoted above, to the account of the creation of the couple: man and woman constitute one being (Gen. 2:24); and in v. 15 ("he asks nothing better, now as before, than to breed a God-fearing race") he appeals to their common destiny of the procreation of children (cf. Gen. 1:28). It is then to this primitive ideal that the couple is to return. There is, however, no doubt that the fidelity of Jahveh towards Israel,

[22] In the same epoch the requirements of the Torah were made stricter as far as foreign wives were concerned by the reforms of Nehemias (2 Esdras 13:1–3; 23–9) and Esdras (1 Esdras 9–10). But the Book of Ruth makes a tactful protest against this severity: Ruth, the stranger, is converted to the true God (Ruth 1:16) and will be the ancestress of David. The same book gives evidence of the practice of levirate to ensure the continuation of the family (Deut. 25:5–10), but this does not spring from the ancient practice of polygamy.

whom he has joined with himself in a *berith,* is implicitly put forward as a model for husband and wife.

The editor of Proverbs (Prov. 1–11) similarly puts forward an ideal in opposition to the illusions of sexual licence. On the one hand the young man is invited to flee the enticements of the strange woman, who is adulterous and corrupting (5:1–14; 7:1–27); she takes the man with her on the road of death, for she does not form a true couple with him, but is merely eager for unbridled lust (cf. the story of Joseph).[23] In contrast, "the bride thy manhood wins for thee" is a refreshing fountain which brings true joy (5:15–19). There is here a sexual morality and a psychology of love which frankly accepts the desires of the flesh (5:19), but which canalizes them towards the bride of the young man, whom he loves. Unity of marriage is presupposed, faithfulness demanded, no rupture of the conjugal bond is envisaged. Similarly the portrait of the perfect woman (Prov. 31:10–31) again makes the point that she is her husband's joy; carnal pleasure is not the only reason, for the text explicitly mentions that her husband is "bound to her in loving confidence" (31:11).

Ecclesiasticus takes up and develops the advice of Proverbs on associating with women (9:1–9) and on self-control in respect of immoderate passions (23:21–38). On this last point he sets out in detail the tyranny of libidinous passions over the man who has abandoned himself to them. Elsewhere he paints

---

[23] Warnings against foreign women are found in Egyptian wisdom literature (see p. 44, note 4) to which there are parallels in the Book of Proverbs (cf. E. Drioton, "Sur la sagesse d'Aménémopé" in *Mélanges bibliques rédigés en l'honneur d'André Robert,* pp. 254–80, which takes up a controversial stand on this point).

parallel portraits of the good wife and the evil woman (25:13 – 26:18). He gives an excellent psychology of feminine virtues and faults as far as they touch upon the success of the ideal marriage, an important element in life. But it is undeniable that the question is seen entirely from the husband's point of view. The writer cannot even desist from some misogynous comments, justifying himself by reference to the account of original sin: "Through a woman sin first began; such fault was hers, we must all die for it" (25:33).

It is possible to look at the whole question from the opposite angle. The ancient Israelite sage to whom we are indebted for the Jahvist sacred history was surely basing his account on a fact of human experience, corroborated, for instance, in the story of Samson and in the maxims of Ecclesiasticus. Anyone reflecting on the significance of woman for man is led to see in her either the best or worst of all things: at times she is the "mate of his own kind" intended for him by the Creator (Gen. 2:18); at times she becomes the temptress who imitates Eve led astray by the Serpent (Gen. 3:6). Every woman oscillates in her relations with men between these two attitudes. Thus the doctrine of Genesis 2–3 goes beyond the stage of abstract thought and acquires an existential significance. It gives meaning to what is everyday experience: for how many bad-tempered women cause their virtuous husbands suffering, as in the case of Job (2:9) and of Tobias the elder (2:14; 10:4–5,7). But, on the other hand, none of God's blessings is greater than a virtuous and beautiful woman, in harmony with the ideal established in the beginning (cf. Ecclus. 26:16–24).

The object of the Book of Tobias is precisely that of presenting a couple who correspond to this ideal and in this lies its impor-

tance for the biblical theology of marriage. Its content is rich
and deserves to be quoted at far more length than is possible
here, so the salient facts must suffice.[24] The marriage of Tobias
and Sara is not simply a human affair. As in the case of Isaac
and Rebecca (Gen. 24:50), it is the Providence of God which
leads the two young people to one another. It is true that their
marriage fits into the legal framework laid down by the law:
Tobias is Sara's nearest relative and according to the law of
endogamy has the first claim on her (Tob. 6:11–13). But their
meeting has a more profound purpose: up till then Sara was
the victim of a demon and it is Tobias who is to save her from
it (Tob. 6:18). The book, in setting forth the problem, uses the
same means of expression as popular demonology and before
we can appreciate the deeper significance of the tale, we have
to go beyond this superficial level which we may otherwise
find confusing. In fact it is less Sara herself who is in the power
of the demon than the men who want to marry her. As a
woman she is an occasion of cupidity and as such a test for
them; in their attitude towards her they reveal what they have
in their hearts and it was because of the wickedness of their
hearts that Sara's previous husbands fell victim to Asmodaeus.
The indications in the recension of the text followed by the
Vulgate are clear on this point: "The fiend has power over such
as go about their marrying with all thought of God shut out of
their hearts and minds, wholly intent on their lust . . ." (6:17).
The deliverance of Sara will be accomplished only when the
man who comes to her has an upright heart and does not

[24] The text of the book has several divergent recensions. That of the
Vulgate follows a Greek version which is noticeably fuller. The principal
additions will be noted as they occur.

himself let in the fiend of lust. The problem raised by the book is basically that of the salvation of the couple. Given the present condition of sinful humanity, every couple is preyed upon by the demonic powers who try to turn them away from the ideal established by God. Anyone who yields to their domination takes the path of death like Sara's first husbands (Tob. 6:14–15). To take the path of life, husband and wife must adopt a different attitude.

The mutual love of Tobias and Sara is to be a chaste love, sanctified by prayer (Tob. 6:18; 8:4–8); and the Vulgate adds that it is sanctified too by a three-day abstinence which attests the couple's control of their desires and the rectitude of their intentions (Tob. 6:18–22). A love of this kind means that in man and wife we see repeated the ideal of the prototype: either that of Genesis 1:27–8, since the purpose of sexual union will be the procreation of children, or that of Genesis 2:18 which their prayer together recalls. Love, fecundity, mutual help: all these aspects of the couple are united in the institution of marriage. The hedonistic conception of love is left behind: "Lord, thou art my witness that I wed this sister of mine not from love of dalliance; only in the dear hope of leaving a race behind me . . ." (Tob. 8:9). Not only does the institution of marriage sanctify love and cover what may be its vulgar features, but the explicit intention of the partners puts it into a religious perspective and integrates it into spiritual life. The basis of the couple's unity is no longer simply the sharing of the marriage-bed, nor even the profound community of their emotional life, but the common sharing of the best that Tobias and Sara possess: their life with God, manifested in prayer. This is why Tobias is able to save Sara (6:18). It is unnecessary to add that polygamy and divorce are out of the question. Without there being, in fact, any allusion to the divine arche-type for marriage – God's covenant with his people seen in its eschatological perfection – we find in the union of Tobias and Sara exactly the same characteristics: unity and fidelity, fecundity, indissolubility.[25] It is merely necessary to put such a work into its doctrinal setting, which is the marriage between God and his people, between Christ and the Church, for it to become a guide for Christian couples.

This brief glance at the texts which present the ideal of the couple in the era of ancient Judaism shows the undeniable spiritual growth which has taken place. Even the ideal couples in Genesis do not attain the level of Tobias and Sara. This ideological advance is accompanied, on the fringe of our era, by a notable institutional evolution.[26] Even though the letter of the Mosaic law remains in force, practice is often far ahead of it. Polygamy is clearly on the decline; the *Damascus Document*,[27] which is Essene in origin, even prohibits it completely, basing its *halakha* on the text of Gen. 1:27, the same that Christ

[25] Here we might mention, too, the fidelity to the deceased spouse practised by the widow Judith, who refuses all remarriage (Judith 16:22). This ideal recurs in the early Church (1 Tim. 5:9).
[26] On the Jewish ideal of marriage, see J. Bonsirven, *Le Judaïsme palestinien au temps de Jésus Christ* (Paris, 1951), vol. II, pp. 207–16; S. W. Baron, *A Social and Religious History of the Jews* (New York, 1952–8), vol. II, pp. 217–41.
[27] The text has been edited and translated by Chaim Rabin, *The Zadokite Documents* (Oxford, 1954). See G. Vermes, *Les manuscrits du Désert de Juda* (Paris–Tournai, 1953), p. 164; A. Michel in A. Vincent, *Les manuscrits hébreux du Désert de Juda* (Paris, 1955), p. 170. According to this text, the three "snares of Belial" by which he lures Israel away from Jahveh are fornication, wealth and sacrilege. Polygamy is included under fornication.

himself later invokes (*Damascus Document IV*, 20–1). The interpretation of the law of divorce itself becomes more restrictive in certain schools of doctors (for instance, the jurisprudence of the school of Shammai at the beginning of our era, in contrast with the bigger school of Hillel). Lastly the sexual morality imposed on men becomes much stricter, especially as regards relations with prostitutes towards which ancient Israel had shown tolerance (Juda and Tamar, Samson, Josue's spies at Jericho, etc.). Essene pietism, which is echoed in the *Testaments of the Twelve Patriarchs*,[28] exalts the virtue of chastity, especially with reference to the patriarch Joseph. Moreover, even if the *Damascus Document* is addressed to married members of the sect, the historian Josephus testifies that some groups of Essenes practised celibacy for the purpose of religious asceticism.[29] This last point, however, goes beyond the scope of our present enquiry which is concerned only with the question of marriage. In this sphere the evolution of ideas and customs leads us to suppose that the prophetical texts in which the symbol of marriage occurs influenced the Jewish community, by whom they were studied and to whom they offered reasons for conversion and hope, and so altered both the community's actual practice and even its conception of the institution, rendering the latter far closer to the primitive ideal described in the two accounts of

[28] The critical problem presented by the *Testaments* is a difficult one to solve. In its present state the work has obviously been touched up and adapted by a Christian hand; the basis, nonetheless, is an Essene one.

[29] *The Jewish War*, II, viii, 120–1; translation in A. Dupont-Sommer, *The Essene Writings from Qumran* (Oxford, 1961), pp. 27–35. The same testimony is found in Philo, *Apologia pro Judaeis*, 14–17, translated pp. 24–26 of the same work, and in Pliny the Elder, *Natural History* V, 17, 4, translated p. 37.

the creation. It is one more step towards the redemption of the couple, this major problem facing a world weighted down by sin since its beginnings.

b. The Song of Songs

The exegesis of the Song of Songs is one of the most controversial points of biblical criticism.[30] Without going into the question in detail, we feel that some comment is necessary before the book can be used in a theological study.

There are three main theories, each of which presents several variants. According to the first, the subject of the book is human love, whether in the form of a collection of epithalamia,[31] a collection of love-songs,[32] or a lyrical drama.[33] According to the second, the text was written specifically in order to celebrate the nuptials of Jahveh and Israel, whether all the details have a doctrinal significance because of the biblical allusions they contain[34] or whether the general theme is merely developed

---

[30] For a general view of the subject it is useful to consult the following: A. Feuillet, *Le Cantique des Cantiques,* series "Lectio Divina" (Paris, 1953), pp. 11–19 (a rapid survey of the principal positions); H. H. Rowley, *The Interpretation of the Song of Songs* (J. T. S., 1937), reprinted in *The Servant of the Lord and Other Essays* (London, 1952), pp. 187–234; A.-M. Dubarle, "Le Cantique des Cantiques (Bulletin critique)" in *Revue des Sciences Philosophiques et Théologiques,* 1954, pp. 92f.; A. Lusseau in Robert and Feuillet, *Introduction à la Bible,* vol. I, pp. 658–62.

[31] J.-P. Audet, "Le sens du Cantique des Cantiques" in *Revue Biblique,* 1955, pp. 197–221.

[32] This is J. Windany's view of the original collection, see *Le Cantique des Cantiques, Poème d'amour mué en écrit de Sagesse* (Tournai-Paris, 1960).

[33] An hypothesis of G. Pouget et J. Guitton, *Le Cantique des Cantiques* (Paris, 1934).

[34] See A. Robert in several articles, the *Bible de Jérusalem* (Paris, 1951) and an as yet unpublished commentary to appear in the series "Études Bi-

with the freedom appropriate to lyric poetry as regards its use of imagery.[35] Finally a third theory distinguishes two stages in the development of the work: a lyric composition depicting human love in a primitive manner and a later interpretation transposing this poetry to use it as a prophetic symbol of marriage.[36] The exegetes' lack of certainty is itself instructive. It shows that in the era of Persian domination when the Song was almost certainly composed or at least put together and edited,[37] the conception of human love must have been merged in some way or other with the transcendental archetype which the

bliques". Also A. Feuillet, *op. cit.*, and in "La formulation d'appartenance mutuelle (II, 16) et les interprétations divergentes du Cantique des Cantiques" in *Revue Biblique,* 1961, pp. 5–38; R. Tournay, "Les chariots d'Aminadab (Cant., VI, 12): Israël, peuple théophore" in *Vetus Testamentum,* 1959, pp. 288–309.

[35] See D. Buzy in the Pirot-Clamer Bible; cf. "L'allégorie matrimoniale de Jahveh et d'Israël et le Cantique des Cantiques" in *Vivre et Penser,* 1945, pp. 77–90.

[36] For example J. Fichtner in *Echter-Bibel, Das Hohe Lied* (1950). J. Windany *(op. cit.)* takes a different line of interpretation in thinking that the original poem was applied secondarily to the metaphorical marriage between Solomon and the Divine Wisdom. A. Feuillet, returning to his earlier position in his 1961 article, admits that there is "a pre-history of the Song" from the literary point of view (*Revue Biblique,* 1961, p. 34). This is my own position approached from a different angle: the love-poems which are chiefly used in the Song were preadapted to express the prophetic theme of the covenant because they were initially concerned with human love.

[37] There is evidence for this in the presence of several Persian words. Aramaic expressions are a less positive indication and need more careful interpretation. The previous oral tradition must, however, be taken into account; cf. J.-P. Audet (*art. cit.,* note 31, pp. 215–18). J. Windany puts back the composition of the text till the 3rd century (under the domination of the Lagids).

prophet has revealed to Israel, whether this archetype was a subsequent addition to poems which simply dealt with human love or whether it was already possible to write a dialogue between Jahveh and Israel in the very realistic language of human love.

My own feeling on the question is that the very realism is an indication that we should not look for the literary origin of the text (at least not in its essentials) among the speculations of wisdom literature on the nuptials of Jahveh and Israel. I find it hard to imagine Israel dreaming of Jahveh and saying in its mystical love: "A kiss from those lips! Wine cannot ravish the senses like that embrace . . ." (Song of Songs 1:2). Even more unlikely are the words of Jahveh dreaming of his union with Israel: "Thy stature challenges the palm tree, thy breasts the clustering vine. What thought should I have but to reach the tree's top and gather its fruit?" (Song of Songs 7:8–9). To have recourse to pure poetry in order to explain these lyrical developments of the prophetic theme, is to evade the many difficulties which the details of the text present. To find throughout subtle allusions to earlier texts, is artificially to fragment a masterpiece of lyric poetry. In its first stages, the Song must have been simply a collection of love-songs. One can regard the poems as connected with the traditional wedding celebrations (cf. 1 Mach. 9:39): "cries of joy and mirth . . . voice of bridegroom and of bride . . ." (Jer. 7:34; 16:9; 25:10) as J. P. Audet has suggested, [38] without being in any way obliged to see the celebrations as a liturgical ceremony: the book of Tobias intimates that after the conclusion of the contract (Tob. 7:16–17) and the taking of the

[38] J.-P. Audet, *art. cit.,* note 31, pp. 211–14.

bride into the bride-chamber (7:19), there were several days of family rejoicings (Tob. 8:20; cf. Judges 14:10–18).

There is, nevertheless, little doubt that the work was the subject of a re-interpretation made necessary by the prophetic symbolism of marriage,[39] a fact attested by the Rabbinic tradition of the second century of our era.[40] It was certainly not an innovation at the time and, although material proof is lacking, one can take it as certain that it was used and interpreted allegorically long before our era.[41] The use of the Song as a liturgical text and its introduction into the list of sacred books must have made its re-interpretation yet more common.[42] In its turn, this would probably have influenced the actual transmission of the text and account for a certain amount of literary adaptation, touching-up and glosses, where the symbolic significance of the imagery is most susceptible to such treatment.[43] The book can

[39] Such re-interpretations are not uncommon in literary history. The educated Chinese of the feudal epoch interpreted the peasant songs of the *Che King* in a moral sense, applying Confucian precepts to them; cf. M. Granet, *Fêtes et chansons anciennes de Chine* (Paris, 1919).

[40] Mishna, *Yadaim,* III, 5 (Aqiba insists on the holiness of the Song); *Taanith,* IV, 8 (Simeon b. Gamaliel II quotes Song of Songs 3:11 interpreting it allegorically). See the quotations from the Mechilta in P. Vuilliaud, *Le Cantique des Cantiques d'après la tradition juive* (Paris, 1925), pp. 61–62.

[41] There is possible evidence for this in the fourth book of Esdras. See 5:24–26 and compare Song of Songs 2:14; 5:14.

[42] There are several possible opinions here: either the use of the collection as a canonical and liturgical book brought with it this learned re-interpretation within the framework of the schools and the readings in the synagogue, or the re-interpretation, after being inaugurated in the scribes' schools, encouraged the systematic liturgical use of the Song.

[43] Here careful analyses, such as those of R. Tournay (*art. cit.,* note 34),

79

therefore be read from two different but closely connected viewpoints: that of human love and that of the divine nuptials of which human love is the symbol. The same thing happened to Psalm 45: initially a royal epithalamium, it suffered the fate of the other royal psalms; having been included in the canonical Psalter after the exile, it was re-interpreted according to prophetical theology and applied to Israel and God or the Messiah.[44] This is not to deny the inspired character of its original form, but its definitive biblical meaning is that intended by the later editors: a transference has been effected from human marriage to the divine nuptials. The same may be said for the import of the Song.

An examination of the text will give some indications of the Jewish conception of the human couple.[45] The aspect of fecundity is hardly mentioned. On the other hand, the love of the Lover and his betrothed is expressed in long lyrical effusions[46] in which all the various aspects of joyous love are blended frankly and with perfect freedom, from discreetly evoked sexual pleasure (1:1–3, 16; 2:6; 4:16–5:1; 7:8–9; 13:14) to the most delicate

prove indispensable for elucidating the intention of the editors. J.-P. Audet does not rule out the re-reading as wisdom literature of an older text (*art. cit.,* note 31, pp. 217–18) but in his opinion the work itself does not bear this out.

[44] Cf. p. 44, note 5. R. Tournay (*Les Psaumes,* Bible de Jérusalem, pp. 199–202) considers it as a late composition, anthological in style analogous to the Song, as he interprets it.

[45] A.-M. Dubarle, "L'amour humain dans le Cantique des Cantiques" in *Revue Biblique,* 1954, pp. 67–86 (an excellent analysis of the text).

[46] Parallels between the Song and Egyptian love-songs have been pointed out by all exegetes. See the texts quoted by P. Gilbert, *La poésie égyptienne* (Bruxelles, 1949), pp. 61–79.

and heartfelt affection. This has led certain critics who favour a naturalist interpretation of the Song to speak of erotic hedonism and find numbers of licentious puns and double-meanings. In doing so, they completely misrepresent the spirit of the work. Without the name of God once being mentioned, everything in human love appertaining to the order of creation is hallowed by implicit reference to a divine norm, part of the Israelitic tradition: the monogamous love of two beings called to become *one flesh* as were the prototype couple. The book is clearly not a theological thesis, but gives us an insight into the psychology of love and the way in which it develops in the biblical climate. The theology of marriage is thus deeply rooted in man's experience and in an atmosphere of optimism and joy it embraces an essential aspect of that experience, which a Cathar spirituality would proscribe as evil. It is striking to observe that in the dialogue between lover and beloved there is not the slightest allusion to the tragedy which threatens all human couples. Such an atmosphere of paradise regained is, of course, very often a characteristic of love-poetry and is merely a way of expressing in concrete terms the inner dreams of every couple. But in a literary context that is as aware of the actual condition of man as is the Bible as a whole, it is not insignificant when a return is made to the original condition of man and woman before the tragedy of Eden and its consequences. The perspective of the text is not towards "impaired" love, such as humanity experiences at present, but towards "redeemed" love saved from itself, of which the Book of Tobias gives us a glimpse.

It would in any case be insufficient to stop our analysis at this aspect of the Song. If it is true that the divine nuptials prefigured in the Mosaic covenant and fulfilled in the eschatological cove-

81

nant are the divine archetype of all human love, they must necessarily appear in the intricacies of a text which presents human love escaping from the imperfections of our sinful human condition. Read from this perspective the Song, taking human love as its starting-point, gives us a glimpse of the mystery of the divine covenant foretold by the prophets,[47] no longer merely in its theoretical aspect, but in its existential reality: the reality of the dialogue of love between redeemed humanity and its God. From this point of view the mystical interpretation of the Song is perfectly correct in principle, even if the allegorical exegesis of all the details in the text, as it was done first in the Synagogue and then by the Church, does more than once seem to be gratuitous and arbitrary. From the moment when love is seen to be the essential basis of the relationship between God and his people, who have been saved from evil, when the same profound

---

[47] In his book A. Feuillet rightly includes a lengthy study of the allegory of marriage in prophetical theology (*Le Cantique des Cantiques,* pp. 140–92). But these texts cannot, in my view, be presented as "the precursors of the author of the Song of Songs": they merely precede the Song's re-interpretation, which is as "biblical" as its original composition as a collection of nuptial songs. Feuillet's final article attempts to find in the prophetic formula of the covenant ("You will be my people and I will be your God") the key to the formula in the Song: "All mine, my true love, and I all his" (Song of Songs 2:16). The *Bible de Jérusalem* makes the same parallel (p. 859, note d). It seems to me, however, that the formula belongs far more to the language of love in all countries and all civilizations; the theme of the covenant is only a secondary feature, because marriage itself is seen as a *berith* (cf. Mal. 2:14). This formula of mutual belonging is implied to a certain extent in 7:10 too, but here the parallel with Gen. 3:16 is striking: "My true love, I am all his; and who but I the longing of his heart?" Here Genesis and the Song of Songs both adopt a formula borrowed from the same language of love.

movement is found analogically in the human couple and in the archetypal couple of which God is one partner, it is easy to understand how the same language can be applied to the human condition restored to its primitive ideal and to the supernatural mystery of which it is the privileged symbol. It is not only a question of a theology of the Church as Spouse, of which the prophets had already provided the skeleton. Behind the fervour of human love the mystical dialogue between God and man is unfolded. It is for this reason that spiritual writers who themselves experience this dialogue almost instinctively have recourse to the text of the Song to find an adequate expression of their intimate relations with God.[48]

It must, however, be emphasized that ancient Judaism, bound by the limitations of the Old Testament, could only provide the bare outlines of such an interpretation of the text.[49] It is only under the brighter lights of the New Testament that the fullness of the text's significance will be appreciated. What is remarkable is the extent to which the work is ideally suited for the purpose of re-interpretation: the experience of human love, understood

[48] Recourse to the language of love to express mysticism is not peculiar to the Christian tradition. In medieval Hindu mysticism the legend of Krishna in love with the shepherdesses is used to translate the relationship between the soul and the divine, cf. L. Renou, in *L'Inde classique,* vol. I (Paris, 1947). But here the symbol is only intelligible in the light of sacred history and the covenant.

[49] The researches of A. Robert, A. Feuillet, and R. Tournay, on the parallelisms which allow the significance of details of the text to be established, are of considerable importance at this point. This is so less because they explain the literary origin of the composition (except for details where the text has been intentionally modified) than because they suggest what were the readings of the ancient Jewish doctors to whom we owe the re-interpretation of the book.

and lived according to the standards of the biblical revelation, was already transfigured by reference to its supernatural archetype even though the complete revelation of this archetype would not be given until that future day when the new covenant was realized in an historical event, when the nuptials of God and humanity were accomplished in the incarnation of the Word. This is the real contribution of the New Testament: with its advent the divine archetype of the couple is no longer a dream or even a promise; it is a reality which has entered the realm of human experience.

III

THE NEW TESTAMENT

ONE WAY of studying the decisive contribution of the New Testament is to examine in turn the different groups of books which are witnesses of revelation. This is the method usually adopted by modern biblical theology. In this way Christ's thought and the theology and practice of early Christianity, of St. Paul and St. John, on the subject which particularly interests us here would be laid bare. In a synthetic study of this sort, there are perhaps better ways of approaching the problem; for instance, to examine, as we shall do, the evidence of the New Testament in its two essential aspects. On the one hand, on a practical level, the Law of Christ, the fulfilment and perfection of the ancient Law (Matt. 5:17), gives the institution of marriage its final perfection, while at the same time proclaiming the superiority of virginity and celibacy: this is the twofold foundation of the whole sexual ethic. On the other hand, the revelation of the mystery of Christ and the Church, the fulfilment of the prophetical promises, gives to this Law its most profound foundation, since the mystery is a nuptial mystery imparting meaning to man's life as a whole, to the institution of marriage and to celibacy as a deliberate vocation.

1. The Law of Christ

Our aim here is not to show how the "Law of Christ" (Gal. 6:2; cf. 1 Cor. 9:21) fulfils the ancient Law either by carrying its precepts to their final perfection or by integrating it into man's spiritual life. Thanks to the gift of the Holy Spirit, charity is the essence and the fulfilment of the Law (Rom. 13:10); it has been "poured out in our hearts by the Holy Spirit, whom we have received" (Rom. 5:5). Here we are concerned only to look more closely at what the Law tells us on the subject of sexuality.

a. Marriage

First of all let us reconsider Christ's words on the subject. To cast light on the question of marriage, Jesus refers his hearers to the original prototype presented in the Creation narrative (Gen. 1:27 and 2:24): in the kingdom of God, which he is inaugurating, the institution of marriage regains the perfection which the consequences of sin in human history had caused it to lose (Matt. 19: 1–9). The latitude permitted by the ancient Law in this respect was "to suit their hard hearts" (19:8); but once the kingdom has been founded, once the economy of grace has been introduced into history, the human couple must return to its primitive rules of conduct, which alone conform to the fundamental intention of the Creator. No reference is made to the problem of polygamy; the authority of Genesis is taken as being sufficient to dismiss the possibility: the two are to become one flesh. From this point of view, the evolution of Jewish customs has already attained a standard which Christ consecrates for all time. There remains the problem of divorce. The way in which Christ's opinion is sought on this subject is reminiscent of debates between doctors: "Is it right for a man to put away his wife, for whatever cause?" The school of Shammai at the time required a grave reason; that of Hillel any reason whatever.[1] The solution which Jesus propounds is not one which had been envisaged by any of the doctors. Taking his stand on Genesis 1:27 and 2:24, he declares: "What God then has joined, let not man put asunder" (Matt. 19:6). Here he is in conscious opposition to the letter of the ancient Law (cf. Matt. 5:31; 19:7–8), because the watch-word of the new Law is a striving for perfection, in imitation of the perfection of God (Matt. 5:48). Any repudiation which is followed by re-marriage must therefore be regarded as adultery (Matt. 5:32; 19:9)[2] and adultery is already strictly prohibited by the Law (Matt. 5:27).

Jesus does not, however, advocate that the punishments laid down by the Law should be carried out; to those who bring before him the woman caught in flagrant adultery he replies: "Whichever of you is free from sin shall cast the first stone at her" (John 8:3–9). His attitude is only surprising if one does

---

[1] J. Bonsirven, Le Judaïsme palestinien au temps de Jésus–Christ, vol. II, pp. 214–16. The question is more fully treated in the work mentioned in the next note.

[2] The clause in Matt. 5:32 and 19:9 (. . . he who puts away his wife, not for any unfaithfulness of hers, and so marries another . . .) has provoked much discussion and sustained a variety of explanations. Christ's argument as a whole excludes the hypothesis of an authorization of divorce in the case of the woman's misconduct, permitting the man's remarriage. Bonsirven (Le divorce dans le Nouveau Testament, Tournai-Paris, 1948) thinks the unfaithfulness refers to a case of illegal concubinage, necessitating the sending away of the woman; such an interpretation remains problematic. There remains the possibility of dismissal of the woman without remarriage, which no text excludes and which 1 Cor. 7:11 explicitly allows, referring to the Lord's precept.

not know the part played by mercy in the kingdom of God: Jesus has not come to call the just (who regard themselves as such) but sinners (who recognize that they are sinners and repent) (Mark 3:15–17; Luke 15; 18:8–14).[3] It is this conversion from the heart that Jesus expects of the woman caught in adultery: "Go, and do not sin again henceforward" (John 8:11). Moreover, the rule of life which he propounds is far more demanding, seen as a whole, than that laid down by the Old Testament, since he stigmatizes even lustful glances and desires as adultery (Matt. 5:27). But his severity is tempered at the same time by a profound understanding of the actual human condition, in which sin has its natural place, since it is a fallen humanity, which divine grace must restore to its original order. Sins of the flesh do not shock Christ. He scandalizes his host, the Pharisee, by receiving a woman who is a public sinner: her repentance is the guarantee of the forgiveness of her sins (Luke 7:36–50). On the other hand, he reproaches the "faithless and misguided generation", whose conduct resembles that of Israel in the time of the prophets, with the scathing words: "The publicans and the harlots are further on the road to God's kingdom than you" (Matt. 21:31–2).

This juxtaposition of an appeal to an absolute ideal and a realistic condescension towards human wretchedness constitutes a paradox which is incomprehensible outside the economy of grace instituted here on earth by the kingdom of God. For our human instinct would be to judge with greater severity the sinners who failed to observe the Law, while interpreting the

[3] The privilege of sinners in the kingdom is stressed by all Gospel commentaries. See for example J. Jeremias, *The Parables of Jesus* (London, 1954), pp. 99–120.

principles with far greater laxity. Scandalized by his indulgence his hearers are astounded when Christ prohibits divorce: "If the case stands so between man and wife, it is better not to marry at all" (Matt. 19:10). In effect, Christ's words are only made intelligible by a gift of God (cf. Matt. 19:11): only by entering the life of the kingdom of God through faith can one perceive both the meaning and purpose of the new Law and the possibility of its being put into practice. It is hardly surprising, therefore, that many of those without faith today remain insensible to this ideal. It is true that it is part of the natural law, since it is no more than a return to the normal order of creation, which was disturbed by human sin. Nonetheless, it is only in the kingdom of God and by his grace that human nature regains its order.

If we turn next to the writings of the apostles, we see that the ideal in question has become the rule of life in the Christian communities. At the level of marriage as an institution, divorce is formally prohibited in accordance with the Lord's command (1 Cor. 7:10–11). The only exception made is in the case of an unbelieving partner who refuses to live with the Christian husband or wife; then the bond between the couple is dissolved, since the new life received from Christ calls in question all the ties which bound the "old man" and frees him from those which, far from being in accordance with the divine order of things, would in fact constitute a tyranny (1 Cor. 7:12–16). But it is not sufficient simply to lay down fundamental principles. The life of married people presents daily concrete problems which demand practical rules.[4] Here they must be guided first

---

[4] This point is dealt with in all the works which treat the theology of St. Paul or the New Testament. See J. J. von Allmen, "Maris et femmes d'après saint Paul" in *Cahiers théologiques,* 29 (Neuchâtel - Paris, 1951).

of all by the general principles which govern the fundamental attitude of husband and wife towards one another (cf. Col. 3:18–19; Eph. 5:21–33; 1 Tim. 2:9–15; 1 Pet. 3:1–7). The texts of Genesis, in presenting the prototype couple are another guide. On the husband's part, the need is for love (Col.; Eph.), respect, understanding of the delicate creature that is woman (1 Pet.). On the wife's part, there is need for submission (Col.; Eph.; 1 Tim.; 1 Pet.), modesty and the other feminine virtues (1 Tim.; 1 Pet.), on the model of the saintly women of earlier times (1 Pet.), care not to be led astray like Eve (1 Tim.), trust in the salvation to be found in child-bearing (1 Tim.). All the heritage of the Old Testament is condensed in these rules, which were probably formulated in connection with the instruction of neophytes.

For those baptized persons who already have experience of Christian life and for whom there is the problem of asceticism within the context of marriage, St. Paul explains how they must integrate sexuality into their Christian life (1 Cor. 7:1–9). Under the influence of Greek spiritualistic thought, for which the things of the flesh were by their nature evil and fettered the life of the soul, they might be tempted to carry out a self-imposed continence (7:1). This would be to ignore the imbalance affecting sexuality in humanity's present state of sinfulness; it would be, too, to forget the duty of the partners one towards the other: having given themselves to one another, they no longer belong to themselves (7:3–4). Continence may be an ideal (we will return to this point), it may have a place in the life of husband and wife as a temporary ascetic measure to encourage the life of prayer, but it would be unrealistic to impose it on everyone (7:5–6). The individual must act according to the state of life in which he finds himself, for God's gifts vary according to the circumstances of each individual (7:7, 17, 20, 24).

Understood in this way conjugal love does justice to the needs of the flesh, without bearing any resemblance to those excesses of eroticism of which the pagan world of the time offered innumerable examples. It is a chaste love, since it presupposes on the part of the husband and wife an attitude that is oblatory and not one that is egoistic (1 Cor. 7:3–4; cf. Eph. 5:25). It is further purified by the measure of asceticism which is introduced into it (1 Cor. 7:5). By canalizing the use of sex, it corrects the natural tendency which draws men to incontinence (1 Cor. 7:2, 5) and rescues them completely from the defiling impurities of which St. Paul has painted such sombre pictures (Rom. 1:24–7; 1 Thess. 4:5; Eph. 4:19). In fact, even after baptism, man remains subject to the desires of the flesh and it is important that he should reject them in order to do the will of God, which is his sanctification (1 Thess. 4:3–7). Nothing is less in keeping with Christian sanctity than sexual irregularities of whatever sort: adultery (1 Thess. 4:4, if such is the meaning of this much-disputed passage[5]) or fornication, which the Greeks of the time regarded with the greatest indulgence (Gal. 5:19; 2 Pet. 2:2). Christian liberty is not to be equated with licence: the body of the baptized person belongs to the Lord, it is a member or limb of the Lord's body; so it would be monstrous for him to unite his body with a prostitute

[5] See the discussion of this passage in B. Rigaux's commentary, "Les épîtres aux Thessaloniciens" in *Études Bibliques,* 1956, pp. 503–6. The writer is of the opinion that the text is concerned with the respect due to the body, rather than that due to the wife.

and so become one flesh with her (1 Cor. 6:12–20). This false couple, united only by a base passion, would degrade and profane the temple of the Holy Spirit which is our body; the true couple, on the other hand, can legitimately use the desires of the flesh, in accordance with Christian precepts, without turning their back on holiness.

Pauline casuistry takes all aspects of the problem into account. The apostle is a realist, who has no illusions about the actual condition of men and women. The baptized have not as yet attained the integrity which will be theirs in paradise; they have only the assurance of it, in the Holy Spirit who has been given to them (2 Cor. 5:2–5; Rom. 8:23); they must work towards it by living according to the Spirit (Gal. 5:16–23) and this presupposes a real crucifixion of the flesh (Gal. 5:24). This principle, applicable to all situations and states of life, is valid for marriage too. The conjugal life should not be imagined as a spiritual idyll in which husband and wife escape *ipso facto* from all evil lust and desires. They too have to "mortify the ways of nature through the power of the Spirit" (Rom. 8:13). The necessity of being dead to one's former nature in order to live in Christ; of having a share in his death in order to share in his resurrection (Rom. 6:1–14), is binding on them even in their married life: their life together will only be that of the "new man" if it has the Cross as its focal point. This asceticism is in no way based on the opposition between body and spirit, in the Greek meaning of the terms. Flesh and spirit, as St. Paul uses the words,[6] characterize the two men which each of us feels within himself (Rom. 7:14–24; 8:1–11): the old man, son of Adam,

[6] See the details of Pauline anthropology given by C. Spicq, *Dieu et l'homme selon le Nouveau Testament,* pp. 147–77.

that makes us the slave of sin; and the new man, reborn in Christ (Rom. 6:1–11). The cross and the resurrection of Christ are present simultaneously in the life of the Christian: the one leads to the other.

b. Celibacy and Virginity

This awareness of man's wretched and sinful condition excludes any purely ascetic conception of continence, such as those might envisage who are carried away by abstract ideals of human perfection. Yet the gospels and the writings of the apostles give an important place to celibacy and virginity; but their approach is entirely different.

First of all, there is the aphorism of Christ, recorded by St. Matthew, which praises the continence of voluntary eunuchs who "have made themselves so for love of the kingdom of heaven" (Matt. 19:12). It is possible that, in the context in which the sentence occurs, it refers in fact to the problem posed by the separation of the marriage partners (cf. 19:9–10);[7] but the implications go far beyond the limits of this particular problem. Seen in the perspective of the kingdom, absolute continence is a good, a greater good even than the lawful use of marriage, for those who have the gift for such a vocation (19:12). Jesus himself practised it and he lived the mystery of the kingdom in all its fullness. To those who would forsake their wife for the sake of the kingdom, he promised that they would be repaid a hundredfold (Luke 18:29–30; the reference is missing from the parallel texts, Matt. 19:27–30 and Mark 10:29–30). Here we have a paradox which needs careful elucidation.

[7] J. Dupont, *Mariage et divorce dans l'Évangile: Matt. 19:3–12* (St-André lès Bruges, 1959).

It is obvious that sexual life is not condemned as evil. It belongs, however, to an imperfect, impermanent order of things, which is destined to disappear: that of the present world (to use a Rabbinical expression). This order of things will be superseded in the world to come. It will vanish from the final fulfilment of the kingdom of God, of which Jesus gives us a glimpse as an addition to the Jewish apocalypses: after the resurrection, "there is no marrying and giving in marriage; they are as the angels in heaven are" (Matt. 22:30). The earthly life of historical mankind is progressing towards this end, which is what justifies its existence. It is in this perspective that the institution of marriage by the Creator is to be understood and its eventual transcendence foreseen. In fact, since the time of Christ's advent among us, the kingdom of God has in a certain sense been present here on earth, at the very heart of history.[8] This is the reason why Jesus restores marriage to its primitive purity; eschatology reintegrates mankind into paradise regained. Voluntary continence anticipates the state into which we will all enter after the resurrection of the body. Seen in this way it has a symbolic function: it attests that the kingdom of God is not only a future reality which will come about on the last day; but that it is also a present reality, since in sexual matters man can already live the mystery in its fullness, in as much as this is possible for the being of flesh and blood that he remains. This is the meaning of Christ's celibacy and those who wish to follow in his footsteps in this respect must give their personal celibacy the same purpose.

There is, nonetheless, a profound difference between Jesus

[8] A. Feuillet in Robert and Feuillet, *Introduction à la Bible*, vol. II, pp. 776–9.

and the eunuchs who "make themselves so" in imitation of him. For him, the transcendence of sexuality (not in essence but in use) is realized at the level of a nature fully in order, "in the fashion of our guilty nature" (Rom. 8:3), but set apart from sin and the lusts which spring from sin, since it is the flesh of the Lamb "so pure, so spotless a victim" (1 Pet. 1:19). For other men this transcendence is something which has to be won in the face of the demands of a rebellious flesh. The fact that this victory can be realized effectively – though not without difficulty and partial failures – is evidence that a new force is at work in man: that of the Spirit of God, which fashions the spiritual man in us and makes us live the life of the kingdom of heaven.

Within the gospels themselves we find a case where virginity and continence have meaning in the light of the kingdom of God: the marriage of Mary and Joseph,[9] the predestined setting for virginal motherhood (Matt. 1:18; Luke 1:27, 34). The mystery of Christ's birth does not belong to the ancient order of things, in which man, conceived in the normal way, was born tainted by sin (this is the sense of Ps. 50:7). It is in every sense part of the new order, that of the kingdom of God, and the virgin birth, implying a continent marriage, is the symbol

---

[9] I do not intend to treat the question of Mary's intention of virginity, which is raised by an exegesis of Luke 1:34. Her vocation to virginity is linked with the annunciation itself by J.-P. Audet, "L'annonce à Marie" in *Revue Biblique,* 1956, pp. 346–74. For the opposite view, see the arguments of R. Laurentin, *Structure et théologie de Luc* 1–2 (Paris, 1957), pp. 176–88: Essene asceticism, however different from Christian asceticism, is proof that an ideal of continence could exist in the Judaism of the time.

of its different allegiance. It is not surprising that non-Christian historians relegate the account given us by Matthew and Luke to the realm of pious legend: as a fact, it is inconceivable and incredible for anyone who does not penetrate by faith the mystery of the Son of God made man, to which the mystery of the kingdom is linked organically. Moreover, early Christian catechesis took the virgin birth as its starting-point when proving the divinity of Christ (cf. the speeches in Acts and Mark's gospel). It is only at a second stage in its development that it viewed the mystery of this birth in the light of the mystery as a whole (cf. Matthew and Luke). Then the virgin birth was revealed not only as intelligible and in accordance with the Scriptures (Isa. 7:14; cf. Matt. 1:22; Luke 1:31), but closely connected with the incarnation and the kingdom of God. This is why in order to present the person of Jesus in concrete terms the evangelists needed this further insight, which Mark's work did not yet possess, even though the surprising appellation "son of Mary" (Mark 6:3) may be a subtle indication in this direction.[10] In any case once the doctrine of the incarnation was understood, the birth of Jesus to a chaste couple took on the symbolic significance shown by both Matthew and Luke.

St. Paul does not, in fact, speculate on this symbol (cf. Gal. 4:4); he seems even to be unaware of Christ's words about

[10] Jesus is called "son of Mary, which means the only son of a widow", writes P. Lagrange, *The Gospel according to St. Mark* (London, 1930), p. 54. On the basis of textual criticism, the authenticity of the expression is questioned by V. Taylor, *The Gospel according to St. Mark* (London, 1952), pp. 299–300, who would be willing to see in it a reference to her virginal motherhood, but thinks that Mark cannot have been familiar with this tradition; instead he suggests a scribal correction, supposing the data given in Luke 1–2 to have been known.

voluntary celibacy (cf. 1 Cor. 7:25). Nonetheless, he has a message to impart about the appropriateness of virginity and celibacy. He himself is celibate, in other words, a eunuch for love of the kingdom (1 Cor. 7:8) and his own experience of voluntary continence, lived in faithfulness to the Spirit of God, is not without influence on the advice he gives to virgins (cf. Cor. 7:25). If marriage is good, celibacy and virginity are better. The married man and woman "will meet with outward distress" (7:28); because they are "concerned with the world's claim", they will be "at issue with themselves" (7:33–4). Paul would wish to see them like himself, completely "concerned with God's claim, asking how they are to please God" (7:32–4). For "the time is drawing to an end" (7:29) and "the fashion of this world is soon to pass away" (7:31). Having regard to the present "times of stress", virginity and celibacy constitute "the best condition for man to be in" (7:26). This is because such a condition is meaningful in terms of the progression of the present world towards its eschatological fulfilment.

It is worth recalling here what Paul says elsewhere: that "the whole of nature, as we know, groans in a common travail all the while" (Rom. 8:22); and we are associated with this travail: "we ourselves, although we have already begun to reap our spiritual harvest, groan in our hearts, waiting for that adoption which is the ransoming of our bodies from their slavery" (Rom. 8:23). This is the condition of the Christian virtue of hope. It longs for the fullness of salvation, since it has already experienced a foretaste of it and so desires the experience in its full perfection. This is the condition of the life of charity. It exists already, but its vision is of a perfection in which everything imperfect will be swept away (1 Cor. 13:10), when God

97

will no longer be a confused reflection in a mirror, but we shall see him face to face and know him as he knows us (1 Cor. 13:12). Voluntary celibacy and Christian virginity anticipate in some sense that future state which is the destiny of all of us and are proof that we already possess its first-fruits (Rom. 8:23; 2 Cor. 5:2–5).

At this point we can understand the significance of perfect continence, adopted for love of the kingdom of God, which follows from Christ's words about voluntary eunuchs: it is an eschatological testimony. The life after the resurrection, into which we will enter at the end of time after we have experienced the death of our earthly bodies, has already begun in a certain sense on this earth. The world in which we live at the moment is thus not the only and final setting in which we have to work out our destiny as men. It contains within itself both the principle of its own destruction (sin which condemns it to the judgment and wrath of God) and the germ of the new universe which will come after it. In these circumstances continence is the better course, even if sexuality, restored to order by the Law of Christ is good when used legitimately, since it has regained the state which God created in the beginning. Even as regards married people, if they place themselves in the exact perspective of their times, the time of pardon; the day of salvation (2 Cor. 6:2), intended for conversion, the time of pilgrimage (1 Pet. 1:17), and of trial (Eph. 5:6; 6:13), the time which is already drawing towards its end (1 Cor. 7:31; 1 Pet. 4:7), it is clearly more fitting that they should live as if they had no wife or husband (1 Cor. 7:29), not taking full advantage of what the world offers (7:31). Voluntary continence is a testimony, an outward and visible sign. Such is its importance and significance in the Church. But, given the condition of man weighed down by sin, it cannot be imposed upon all. It must only be adopted prudently: "better to marry than to feel the heat of passion" (1 Cor. 7:9). There is a spiritual call, a gift of the Spirit which is not granted to all (1 Cor. 7:4). Christ himself said so: "That conclusion cannot be taken in by everybody, but only by those who have the gift" (Matt. 19:11). "Each of us", says St. Paul, "has his own endowment from God, one to live in this way, another in that" (1 Cor. 7:7). It is a question of a personal vocation and a right distinction between spiritual gifts.

Virginity and celibacy on the one hand and Christian marriage on the other react upon one another and influence each other. Both belong to the same order of truths: that of the kingdom of God, of redeemed creation, which has a vision of its eschatological fulfilment but has not yet finally reached it, a vision of its absolute liberty which it does not fully possess. Both have their source in the same life in the Spirit, both to a different degree and in different ways. Seen from outside it might appear that one fulfils human nature, while the other sacrifices it. In fact, marriage corrects nature by introducing it into the new world of grace, while celibacy introduces nature into that world in order to consecrate it completely to it. If these two aspects of the question are not fully appreciated, there is a great risk either that marriage will be despised in the name of an inhuman and illusory purity or that celibacy and virginity will be rejected in the name of marriage which is extolled to the point of abuse; as if, on the one hand, marriage was something evil or now completely transcended,[11] or as if, on the other hand, virginity was

[11] This is the Manichean position, taken up again by the Albigensians in the Middle Ages. It has been convincingly argued that this conception

useless and marriage sufficient in a world restored to the perfection of the original Eden.[12] The Christian conception of sexuality exorcizes both these errors, since it is aware both of the reality of life in the Holy Spirit and the real wretchedness of the human situation, in which this life must in fact be lived.

2. The Mystery of the Union of Christ and the Church

We will now consider again the paradox for man and woman which is constituted by the transition from a natural condition, in which their impaired sexuality is in a state of imbalance, to the life of the Christian couple and, even more, to voluntary continence. Experience of the human condition is such that many, with apparent logic, regard the gospel ideal as a chimera and, to the extent that it takes the form of a law, even as an unacceptable tyranny. But Christian doctrine is not blind to the conditions under which such an ideal must be realized. Its appreciation of the original human dilemma and its consequences goes far beyond that of the Old Testament, for the

influenced the theory of courtly love, in which there is a distinction between the institution of marriage and the love of the chosen Lady. The influence of this conception, source of the theme of hopeless love, on French literature can be seen from *Tristan et Yseult* to the *Soulier de Satin* (but Claudel takes it up in a genuinely Christian perspective).

[12] Sometimes conjugal spirituality is exalted to such an extent that it threatens the balance of a whole in which marriage and celibacy complement one another. Luther's position is very different: if he extols Christian marriage and denounces the illusions of celibacy, it is because of the weakness of man and the existence of marriage as *remedium concupiscentiae*. His revolt against celibacy, explicable by the personal drama into which he was thrown by a doubtful monastic vocation, finally causes him to sacrifice an essential aspect of Pauline theology.

redemptive act of Christ has revealed the depth and extent of man's fall. It therefore sets forth firmly as a fundamental principle, that man would not by his own powers be capable of fully attaining the ideal of marriage or voluntary continence: the miracle of redemptive grace is needed. Only this grace can create the new man by totally renewing his whole being (Eph. 4:22-24; cf. Ps. 50:12). By remedying in·this way the natural injury which befell man's sexuality[13] like all the other aspects of his being, it makes possible both the sanctification of the couple and a renunciation of the use of sex which will involve neither degradation nor a lack of balance in man.

But on a closer consideration of the conditions in which this miracle of grace takes effect, an intrinsic link with sexuality is not at all obvious. Surely grace is of a purely spiritual order, while sexuality, although it colours the whole human personality, belongs essentially to the physical order?[14] Such an over-simplified explanation is inadequate. In reality the mystery of Christ which effects mankind's redemption is the mystery of a union,

[13] It is essential not to imagine this medicinal action of grace in an over-simplified form. Man is not thereby restored to a state of integrity analogous to that which theology attributes to Adam before his fall. He is merely given the power of combating efficaciously, on the moral plane, the irregular inclinations which persist in him until his death. See for instance M. J. Scheeben, *The Mysteries of Christianity* (London, 1954). The power of this grace "finds its full scope in weakness" (2 Cor. 12:9). Its action leaves a clear field for the use of medical means which may, at their own level, obviate this "weakness". But medicine would scarcely be able to calculate its effects exactly, if it was unaware of the spiritual aspect of the problem.

[14] Here we are taking the words flesh and spirit not in the sense they are used by St. Paul, but in that of Greek philosophy and modern anthropology.

in which God and mankind are face to face in the rôles of bride-groom and bride. The life of the new man regenerated by grace, the marriage of two baptized persons, and continence observed "for love of the kingdom of God" are all equally a participation in this mystical union which is both their basis and the source of their meaning.

At this point we come back to what has already been said about the prophetical symbol of marriage. The prophets revealed the existence of a divine archetype of the couple: the covenant between God and men, realized in the first place in an imperfect form as the Mosaic covenant, awaited in its perfect form as the eschatological covenant. With Christ this eschato-logical covenant became a fact. It is true that we still await its consummation beyond the limits of time, of the present world, of history. But having occurred at the heart of history, as the act above all others in which earth and heaven, the human and the divine, time and eternity meet – for this is the meaning of Christ's death followed by his resurrection (Mark 14:24; Matt. 26:28; Luke 22:20; 1 Cor. 11:25; Heb. 8:6–10, 17) – this new and eternal covenant introduced into the world a principle of transformation which recreates it in its own image, so to speak. The divine archetype of the couple is therefore no longer that of the pagan mythologies, a mere mental personification, invented by men to account for the sacral nature of sex, of which they had an intuitive or instinctive knowledge and which they sought to explain to themselves. It is no longer, as in the Old Testament, a shadow which shares the imperfections of the actual human condition, or a simple promise. It is a fact, the central fact of history, in which a mysterious reality is both fulfilled and revealed, a reality which embraces in its fullness the relationship between man and God. It is in this perspective that the adoption of the prophetical symbolism by the New Testament texts must be seen.

a. Examination of Texts

This nuptial symbolism is used by Christ and reported in some passages preserved by the Synoptics. To the Pharisees who are questioning him about the fact that his disciples do not fast, Jesus replies, "Can you expect the men of the bridegroom's company to go mourning, while the bridegroom is still with them? No, the days will come when the bridegroom is taken away from them; then they will fast" (Matt. 9:15; Mark 2:19–20; Luke 5:34–5). Associated with Jesus by their faith in the gospel, the disciples have therefore entered into the nuptial mystery of the kingdom, inaugurated here on earth at his coming. This mystery has not yet attained its final perfection, since the bridegroom has to be taken away and the time of his physical disappearance will be one of penance. It is not only the deprivation of the Passion which springs to mind here,[15] but that of the Ascension too, which dominates the whole of the Church's economy of time: Christ, the bridegroom, will only be restored to his friends on the day of his return in glory.

The same symbol recurs as a simile in Matthew's version of the wedding-feast parable: the kingdom is not simply compared

---

[15] From the critical point of view it is possible that the second part of the parable (Mark 2:20) is a secondary development which proves its allegorization in the early Church. Cf. J. Jeremias, *The Parables of Jesus,* p. 42, n. 82. This would at least show how the Church of apostolic times interpreted the parables of Jesus in the light of the Passion and the Resurrection.

103

to a feast, as in Luke (Luke 14:16–24; cf. Matt. 8:11); it is the feast which the king makes for the marriage of his son. If it is borne in mind that the king represents God (cf. Matt. 25:34–40) and that Son is one of Christ's titles (cf. Matt. 21:37–38 and passim), the conclusion is inescapable that the parable of the wedding-feast compares the kingdom, in its deepest and most profound sense, to the nuptial mystery in which Christ is the bridegroom.[16]

Finally the parable of the ten virgins (Matt. 25:1–13) takes up the same theme, but goes beyond the wedding-feast (25:10), putting more emphasis on the person of the bridegroom: they are waiting for him, he is long in coming, then he arrives, the virgins who are ready escort him in, the others he does not recognize. The bride is not mentioned, although the virgins are clearly her attendants (cf. Ps. 45:15–16; Song of Songs 2:7, etc.); it is in this capacity that they share in the joy of the wedding, like the "men of the bridegroom's company" mentioned earlier. The problem which is presented here is that of the preparation which is necessary before any participation in this joy, the symbol of the kingdom in its perfect consummation. A time of trial and waiting necessarily precedes it; during this time it is essential to be prudent and not heedless.[17] Here is recalled the present

[16] As in the previous case, we possibly have here the adaptation which the parable underwent in the framework of primitive Christian catechesis. From Luke to Matthew there is the same fundamental meaning, but in Matthew there can be seen the beginnings of an allegorization which extends the original scope of the text. Cf. J. Jeremias, *op. cit.,* p. 53.

[17] The application of the parable to the theme of vigilance (cf. Thess. 5:1–11) is a secondary characteristic: the virgins are not blamed for having fallen asleep (they all did so), but for not having provided themselves with oil.

condition of man, called to the absolute joy of the kingdom but subject to the trials of actual living. The fact that, in the interplay of symbols, those who are waiting for the bridegroom and who go into the wedding-feast are described as virgins is doubtless far from accidental. Without wishing to allegorize the parable in the manner of Gregory the Great,[18] it is permissible to suppose that the mystery of virginity in the Church is here discreetly indicated.[19] There are other examples which corroborate this interpretation.

In St. Paul the essential development of the marriage symbolism is to be found in the epistle to the Ephesians (5:21–32).[20] Closely linked with rules for everyday life which have their parallel in other epistles (Cor. 3:18; 1 Pet. 3:1–7), this letter establishes a bridge between the doctrine of marriage on the one hand and the mystery of Christ and the Church on the other. The human couple has not only a primitive prototype on which

[18] Homily in the Roman Breviary at the Common of Virgins, 1st schema.

[19] From the critical standpoint, such a suggestion is more in keeping with the interpretation of the parable in Christian catechesis (at a time when virginity had become a sort of institution) than with its basic meaning, adapted to Christ's first hearers. According to J. Jeremias, it is the whole Messianic application of the parable that is a secondary allegorization (op. cit., pp. 41–2). If this is so, it is at the level of Christian catechesis that the theme of Christ the bridegroom is here developed.

[20] On this passage see the excellent commentary of H. Schlier, Der Brief an die Epheser (Düsseldorf, 1958), pp. 258–80; the origin of the "sacred marriage" of Christ and the Church is the subject of a long digression, pp. 264–76. The text is put into context as part of Pauline theology as a whole by J. de Baciocchi, "Structure sacramentaire du mariage" in Nouvelle revue théologique, 1952, pp. 917–21; J. J. von Allmen, Maris et femmes d'après St. Paul, pp. 27–39.

to model itself (Eph. 5:31; cf. Gen. 2:24): this prototype itself prefigured the model Couple, which is Christ and the Church. The symbolic interpretation of the person of Adam, "the type of him who was to come" (Rom. 5:14) is germane to such a comparison. What the first Adam was for all men in the order of earthly life, of the activity of the senses, of the psychic body, Christ, the second Adam, is for them in the order of celestial life, of spiritual activity, of the transfigured body (1 Cor. 15:44–9). As the principle of life for his line, Adam has handed on to it at the same time the defects which his sin had introduced into the world (Rom. 5:15–17). As the principle of the new life for humanity as a whole, Christ has given mankind a share in his resurrected state (Rom. 5:15, 18–21; 6:5–11; 1 Cor. 15:49; Eph. 4:23–4). Face to face with Christ, who renews its whole being, the human race is in the position of woman face to face with man and Christ acts towards it as the bridegroom does towards his bride: "Christ shewed love to the Church when he gave himself up on its behalf. He would hallow it, purify it by bathing it in the water to which his word gave life; he would summon it into his own presence, the Church in all its beauty, no stain, no wrinkle, no such disfigurement; it was to be holy, it was to be spotless" (Eph. 5:25–7). In order to become the pure bride of Christ in this way, the human race needed first to be transformed by him; he has made of the sinner, formed in the mould of Eve, a holy virgin. This is the first miracle of his nuptial love, which demanded on his part the surrender of self even to the final sacrifice. The love of the bridegroom is a redemptive love (cf. Tob. 6:18; Osee 3:2–3; Ezech. 16:6–14; 62–3; Isa. 54:6–8) which is consummated in a union in which the bride becomes "his own body" (Eph. 5:28–31).

Sexuality, which belongs to the order of natural creation, does not find the true basis of its sacral character at this level alone. Even its first prototype had as its point of reference a higher reality, which would enter the sphere of human experience at "the appointed time" (Gal. 4:4). There is too the Pauline doctrine which makes Christ, the image of the invisible God, the first-born of all creation: "In him all created things took their being, heavenly and earthly, visible and invisible; what are thrones and dominions, what are princedoms and powers? They were all created through him and in him; he takes precedence of all, and in him all subsist. He too is that head whose body is the Church" (Col. 1:15–17). We see now this principle applies to man; not to man in the abstract, but to the human couple that God created in his "own image and likeness" (Gen. 1:26–7) and that gives concrete existence to human nature in making two into one flesh (Gen. 2:24).

From the very beginning the importance of the couple extended far beyond the sphere assigned it by the psychology and metaphysics of love, both of which are restricted by a natural order obscured and corrupted by sin. It was even then a parallel of the mystery in which the relationship between God and men is realized in all its fullness. What man can mean for woman is what the Word of God pre-eminently means for mankind, created and redeemed by him. What woman means for man, mankind (and so all created being) means for the Word of God, its Creator and Redeemer. It is not by chance that religious symbolism everywhere has recourse to the image of femininity to depict the creature face to face with God, she who is not face to face with Him who is, the desiring Beloved with the absolute Lover. The symbol is corrupted in the mythologies more than once, because the human couples only present a distorted image of their supernatural archetype.[21] Nonetheless, the symbol is written into creation itself, although the archetype which underlies it is an event in time: the incarnation of the Son of God, in which human nature – and with it every creature – is involved by its Creator in an indissoluble union of love.

A few passages in St. John's writings also take up in their turn this nuptial symbol. In the gospel, words of John the Baptist are quoted which sum up the respective situations of Christ and his precursor: "The bride is for the bridegroom; but the bridegroom's friend, who stands by and listens to him, rejoices too, rejoices at hearing the bridegroom's voice; and this joy is mine now in full measure" (John 3:29). Similarly the account of the marriage-feast at Cana certainly has a symbolic background which exegesis can elucidate.[22] For the Jewish water of purifica-

---

[21] We mentioned earlier the case of Hindu tradition (p. 83, note 48). Its mystical interpretation of the myth of Krishna, symbol of the human soul in its love for God, cannot obviate the fact that the myth itself has recourse to the most violent erotic images, such as are displayed on the bas-reliefs of the temple of the sun at Konarak. Here the influence of fertility cults can be seen. The union of man and the divinity remains equivocal in conception: is it in fact a union with the unique personal God, which will achieve man's spiritualization, or an obscure communion with the vital forces which drag human beings into their whirlwind and which are particularly manifest in human sexuality? It is only through the revelation of its true archetype, the couple Christ–Church, that the symbol can be given its authentic meaning.

[22] On this symbolic background, see M. E. Boismard, *Du baptême à Cana (Jean 1:19 à 2:11)*, series "Lectio Divina", 18, pp. 137–43; A. Feuillet, "L'heure de Jésus et le signe de Cana" in *Ephemerides Theologicae Lovanienses*, 1960, pp. 5–22; J. P. Charlier, *Le signe de Cana* (Bruxelles, 1959). The liturgy admirably presents the interweaving of the themes: "Hodie coelesti Sponso juncta est Ecclesia, quoniam in Jordane lavit Christus

tion, bound up with the economy of the old covenant, Jesus miraculously substitutes excellent wine – wine which will later become the symbol of the new covenant in his blood. It is not merely by chance that the theme of the covenant runs through every episode which has a wedding feast as its setting.

Finally, in the Apocalypse, the fulfilment of the covenant outside time in an atmosphere of paradise regained (Apoc. 21:3–4) is explicitly described as the wedding of the Lamb. The psychology of love has no longer any place. The sacred ceremony of marriage alone is evoked in hieratic terms, when the bride in her finest array is presented to her bridegroom (21:2, 9). This feminine embodiment of redeemed humanity is also a city, the same image as was used by the prophets: the new Jerusalem (21:2, 10–27; cf. Ezech. 40ff.; Isa. 54; 60–2), mother of all redeemed men (cf. Gal. 4:26).[23] The description of the Lamb as "slain in sacrifice" (Apoc. 5:6) is a reminder that he shed his blood to obtain salvation for men (5:9–10; 7:13; cf. Eph. 5:25–6). To these eschatological nuptials, at which the bride as a pure virgin is dressed in "linen of shining white" (19:7–8), are bidden

ejus crimina; currunt cum muneribus magi ad regales nuptias, et ex aqua facto vino laetantur convivae" (Benedictus antiphon at Lauds on the feast of the Epiphany).

[23] Opposite the Virgin-Bride, the logic of the symbols puts another city: Babylon, the prostitute with whom all the kings of the earth fornicate (Apoc. 17). Prostitution is here a symbol of idolatry (cf. Osee 1–2). But whereas the Virgin-Bride is mother of the elect, the great harlot is merely the seductress of the reprobate (cf. 18:3). The ambivalence of woman for man is here reproduced symbolically: on the one hand, Virgin, Bride and Mother; on the other, the "strange woman" (cf. Prov. 7) who draws man into her clutches and sets him on the road of death.

all the elect (19:9), who are themselves virgins (14:4). Taking part in the wedding-feast (19:9; cf. Matt. 22:1), they possess eternal happiness (7:15–17). The interplay of metaphors here recalls the imagery both of the Old Testament and of the gospel parables. But the nuptial mystery of the kingdom of God is envisaged less in its sacramental presence during the time of the Church on earth, than in its final fulfilment which will take place after the resurrection of the body.

b. Life in the Mystery

The nuptial mystery of Christ and the Church is not an other-worldly reality, completely beyond our grasp. Even now we are linked with it and have a part in it by faith. It is from our participation in it that the rules of conduct which govern our day to day existence spring, the morality of Christian marriage, the ideal of consecrated celibacy. On these three points St. Paul provides the most explicit texts.

Because he is a member of Christ's Body, of the Church, Christ's Bride, the Christian has been purified like her by bathing "in the water to which his word gave life" (Eph. 5:26). Rescued from the corruption of sinning humanity, that adulterous and wanton bride, the Christian now participates in the virginity of the Church, restored by redemptive grace. In this sense he is a virgin (Apoc. 14:4). This is echoed in St. Paul's words to the faithful at Corinth: "I have betrothed you to Christ, so that no other but he should claim you, his bride without spot" (2 Cor. 11:2). This state will not, however, be fixed once and for all until after death; until then man is constantly tempted and tried by the manifestations of his "guilty nature" (Rom. 8:3), of his "nature thus doomed to death" (Rom. 7:24). Paul continues on the same theme: ". . . and now I am anxious about you. The serpent beguiled Eve with his cunning; what if your minds should be corrupted, and lose that innocence which is yours in Christ?" (2 Cor. 11:3).

The trial of our present existence is thus that of the choice between two basic attitudes: on the one hand, the fidelity which has as its archetype the Church, bride of Christ; on the other hand, the perversity of Eve, corrupted and corrupting, which lives again in all her children when they follow the natural inclination of their perverted instincts.[24] The fidelity in question goes beyond the level of the natural moral life, for it manifests itself above all in the virtues of faith, hope, and charity (1 Cor. 13:13). It includes, however, the practice of all the moral commandments, which are summed up in the virtue of charity (cf. Rom. 13:10). Consequently it involves a requirement of chastity which puts sexual morality into the "nuptial" perspective of the giving of oneself to Christ: "the man who unites himself to a harlot becomes one body with her" but he profanes a member of the body of Christ; "whereas the man who unites himself to the Lord becomes one spirit with him" (1 Cor. 6:16–17).

This way of explaining spiritual life shows clearly that at its most elementary level as well as at its mystic peaks, it is a nuptial mystery. Every Christian lives this mystery on his own account,

---

[24] In the Apocalypse we are given a choice between the attitude of the sons of the Church-Bride, who share in her virginity, and that of the "kings of the earth" who fornicate with the "great harlot" (Apoc. 17:1). For the feminine symbols inspired by the archetype Christ-Church are substituted masculine symbols with an identical significance.

111

not in the ethereal peace of a superterrestrial life, but in the interior struggles of a conscience torn between the desires of the flesh and the will of the spirit (Gal. 5:16–17; Rom. 7:14–25). The tragedy of love, which the prophets had already recognized in the history of Israel recurs in the life of every man. This is why the ancient texts which evoke the tragedy of the people of God have a perpetual relevance: they shed light on the life of every individual. In the story of Israel called to her nuptials, then in turn unfaithful, punished, repentant, purified, pardoned, restored to grace, finally called again to enjoy beatifying union with the heavenly bridegroom, everyone can recognize his own experience. Not an experience made once and for all and henceforth dismissed as finished, but an experience which constantly repeats itself. For the life of the Christian begins with entry into the divine covenant, just as the history of Israel begins with the Mosaic covenant, and has as its final horizon the return to paradise foretold by the prophets when they described the eschatological covenant. But the intermediate era is characterized by a constant oscillation, the sinful condition of man making itself felt in the life of the Christian, just as it did in an earlier era in the life of the people of God. By listening to the existential resonances of the texts, anyone reading the sacred books can find something relevant to his own situation. Mystics will favour the pages which describe the splendour of nuptial love (such as the eschatological promises of the prophets or the Song of Songs[25]). Theologians will follow suit, either in order to understand a

[25] This explains the place of commentaries on the Song in the mystical literature of Christianity from Origen to St. Bernard and the Spiritual Canticle of St. John of the Cross. Cf. p. 83.

mystical experience which they do not necessarily share, or to depict the ideal of life in the Church, the holy bride left unblemished by the sins of her sons. As for ordinary sinners, they will be more likely to turn to the texts which describe the persevering and merciful love of God (Osee, Ezechiel 16) and will find in the eschatological promises foundation for a hope stronger than their consciousness of human wretchedness. In any case, everyone will learn in this way to see himself with regard to God in the position of the bride, loved although undeserving, redeemed and called to the happiness of mutual love.

As far as the Christian morality of marriage is concerned, the relation between the sacramental institution and the nuptial mystery which is its archetype explains the rule of perfection which is henceforward binding on the couple. The respective attitudes of Christ and the Church determine those of the husband and wife (Eph. 5:21–32), since the conjugal union represents and signifies the whole mystery, introducing a sacral value even into its physical consummation.[26] Created in a certain order which was destroyed by sin, this union is recreated in Christ at a level of perfection which it could only attain with the help of

[26] It is clearly important not to confuse the different planes. The physical union, integrating the obscure powers of the life-force, is on the level of interpersonal relationships, not the level of the immediate relationship of the persons with God. Sexual pleasure has meaning in the light of the mystery of Christ, but it is in no way mystical in nature. The exaltation of the senses, which played an essential rôle in the orgiastic mysticisms derived from the fertility cults, is, in Christian mysticism, nothing more than a sign of natural weakness which runs the risk of obstructing the union with God, if it encroaches upon the demands of the divine Spirit. See in this connection: St. John of the Cross, *The dark night of the soul*, Book 1, chap. 4.

redemptive grace. The marriage partners still have to bear with the profound defects left in sexuality by sin. They will learn to know their moral weaknesses. They will know too the bitterness of both willing lapses and almost involuntary falls from grace in the face of apparently insoluble problems (for instance, the problem of limiting births in a Christian family). In short they will be aware that, even if sexuality is in principle sanctified by the sacrament, it still remains difficult to mortify the flesh in order to live according to the spirit (Rom. 8:13). In spite of these drawbacks of a rebellious nature, their sexuality, taken up into a supernatural order which relates it to the mystery of Christ and the Church, will, nonetheless, be saved from the wretchedness which it may still feel, but which is overcome by the medium of grace. In this way a communion of love will be realized between the husband and wife which will restore for them the lost human unity, not in a perfect sense, since there will still be lapses, but, nonetheless, in a real sense, because they have together been joined to God: even physical love will be encompassed by charity.

Here too a Pauline text expresses the ideal to which the Christian couple aspire: "All you who have been baptized in Christ's name, have put on the person of Christ; no more Jew or Gentile, no more slave or freeman, no more male or female; you are all one person in Jesus Christ" (Gal. 3:27–8). Human unity remains the aim (immediate, not simply ultimate) of all society. The diversity of the human race is operative in many different perspectives: those of nations and languages (in other words, cultures), social class, sex. In fallen mankind this diversity is affected by the injury of sin. Instead of being expressed in complementary terms which would tend towards harmonious communion, it shows itself in the dialectic opposition of nations, cultures, classes and sexes.[27] Such internal tensions, inherent in the present condition of the human race, are evidence in their own way of the unity which is lost and looked for; but at the same time, they are an obstacle to its realization. Christ alone gives mankind the possibility of overcoming these dialectical oppositions by restoring the unity of men in the mystery of his Body, his Church who is also his bride: at the transcendental level of supernatural communion they find once again the natural unity which remains the deepest desire of their nature. The fact that in the above-mentioned text St. Paul explicitly mentions male and female shows that the principle is not one which applies only to the problem of conflicting nationalisms, racial or cultural antagonisms, class struggles. It applies with equal force to that elementary society, man and wife. Man and wife too search for an impossible unity through the tortuosities of a dialectic in which man acts the part of master towards the woman–slave: "Thou shalt be subject to thy husband; he shall be thy Lord" (Gen. 3:16). Unless, reversing the rôles, the woman–mistress forces her subjugated lover to his knees. In the sacrament of marriage Christ comes to give back this lost unity to the couple; for their mutual love in Christ, won in spite of resistance from the egoistic flesh, replaces the tensions which they inherited from their guilty nature, the legacy of the first Adam and the first Eve. For the lusts of the old man is substituted the charity of the new

[27] There is moreover an internal relationship between the different aspects of this dialectic, which is the motive power in history. See the studies of G. Fessard, *De l'actualité historique,* vol. I (Paris, 1959), pp. 159–211 (although certain of the writer's systematizations may be exaggerated).

115

man. It is a difficult victory, constantly in jeopardy, which demands a daily fidelity to redemptive grace.

The nuptial mystery of Christ and the Church is translated for a second time into the terms of an institution, a more perfect one than marriage, in the case of virginity and celibacy embraced for love of the kingdom of God. Total abstention from the use of sexuality not out of contempt, or impotence, or fear, but through self-mastery and renunciation, has as its most profound purpose, that of being an eschatological witness. It affirms the actual presence of the mystery in time. It translates the situation, which is that of every Christian, of the "bride without spot" betrothed to Christ (2 Cor. 11:2), into terms of the flesh. It is in a special sense a participation in the condition of the Church herself, spouse and virgin. In this case it is no longer the rightly ordered sexuality of man and wife which represents the mystery of Christ. It is the consecration of sexuality by a human person who thus integrates his whole life with that of Christ, the bridegroom.

We must recognize that the duality of Christian marriage and a celibacy dedicated to God presents a difficult problem of co-ordination, even if their common point of reference to the same supernatural archetype is accepted in principle. Light is thrown on this whole question if it is related to an anthropological problem, with which it has much in common. Human nature has an integrating action on the individuals of either sex, raising them to an equal dignity as persons "in the image and likeness of God" (Gen. 1:26–7). In each case, however, the action works differently, according to different, irreducible, complementary methods, so that the totality of human nature can only be expressed by the human communion of the couple, created as such in the image of God. The sacrament of marriage shows that the human couple is called to reproduce the image of its supernatural archetype and so to sanctify in this way its existence as a couple. Celibacy and virginity, lived in Christ Jesus, show that people of both sexes are called to live, on equal terms, in the mystery through which the regenerated human race approaches God's presence: the mystery of Christ and the Church. To them may be applied, in another sense, the Pauline principle already quoted: "... no more male and female; you are all one person in Jesus Christ" (Gal. 3:28). In the present state of the world, when mankind is emerging from its animal nature while retaining some links with it, the difference between the sexes is an element indispensable to the existence of our race. Against that, when we reach the eschatological fulfilment which will take us into the world to come, this differentiation will lose its validity, since human beings will be called to live the mystery of love in its fullness. But the interior call to this overcoming of sexuality sounds even now, in this world, in the conscience of certain individuals. "That conclusion cannot be taken in by everyone, but only by those who have the gift" (Matt. 19:11); for "each of us has his own endowment from God, one to live in this way, another in that" (1 Cor. 7:7).

It remains true that this gift and this vocation, accepted in the frailty of a "sinful nature", only have meaning and can only be realized in practice within the framework of a life entirely dedicated to Christ, the bridegroom. In such a case they lead the man or woman to unite all the powers of their being in their exclusive gift of self to the eternal bridegroom. They make this act into a state of Christian perfection, which confers on them a privileged position in the Church, without prejudicing the sacramental and sanctifying power of marriage. In return, their life in this state is entirely dependent upon their giving themselves to Christ, though it is not free from sufferings and partial failures.[28] But it must be borne in mind that here, as in marriage, suffering and failure can be meaningful. They remind man of his condition as a creature, fallen and saved by grace, who has nothing to pride himself on when he faces Christ the Saviour. In this way suffering and failure foster true humility and hope in the soul, without which we could not in any way live the nuptial mystery of Christ and the Church.

[28] The above comments on the sufferings and partial failures of souls who have taken the vow of celibacy do not touch on the problem of discerning true vocations. A vocation is not authentic if there is not a reasonable and well-founded hope that the person concerned will adjust himself normally in the celibate state. If this is not the case, neither his own wishes nor the call of some authority will make up for natural deficiencies which are the sign that a real vocation is lacking. It remains true, however, that entering upon a vocation, like entering into marriage, involves some normal risks for the future; for those in the celibate as well as those in the married state, life on earth retains all its trials and temptations.

IV

CONCLUSION
THE HUMAN COUPLE: IMAGE OF GOD

In our attempt to trace through the texts of both the Testaments the doctrine relating to the human couple, as presented
there and progressively developed, we have restricted ourselves to those passages alone in which the couple as such appears,
either in its human reality or in its transcendental archetype:
Jahveh and his people, Christ and his Church. It must by now
be clear that the idea of an archetype was fundamental to this
theology of the couple, since it provided a basis for establishing
the sacredness of the institution of marriage, imposed on it its
essential structure, and dictated the attitudes to be adopted by
the marriage partners.

In the course of our investigation, we took the word archetype in two very different senses. To begin with, the analysis
of pagan myths showed us that, in order to hallow everything
connected with sexuality, ancient man assigned divine archetypes to its various aspects. These were mental archetypes,
which it was important to study in order to understand the men
who coined them, since, according to psychologists, these
archetypes are a direct product of existential experience and
condition the whole psychic life.[1] But later on we saw the advent

[1] Cf. supra, p. 16, note 5. Our concept of the archetype is, however,

of an entirely different type of archetype, resulting from the historical experience of Israel, and in it the diverse aspects of sexuality regain their vital unity: this was the covenant between God and men, initiated on Sinai in an imperfect form, realized in full in the eschatology. This time we had a real archetype, one which the light of reason alone could not disclose, but immediately intelligible from the moment God revealed it to men. The transition from mythical archetypes to this revealed archetype forced us to alter our perspective. From the realm of the psychologists, who study the spontaneous functioning of the mental mechanism without being able to pronounce absolutely on the value of its minutiae, we passed to that of the theologians who know the objective value of divine revelation by faith and who, in consequence, know how to find in the living God archetypes for all created things. Some readers may have been tempted to suspect the influence of Platonism on Christian theology here. They would be mistaken. Plato's use of exemplars is based upon mental archetypes similar to those from which the mythologies were derived. The biblical use of exemplars is based on the certain knowledge that God 'created man in his own image and likeness" (Gen. 1:26); but it is in the historical experience of the people of God, the manifestation of the plan of salvation, that it looks for the necessary criteria to correct, complete and order the archetypal data furnished by everyday experience.[2] This fact is particularly in evidence where the theology of the couple is concerned.

independent of the systematizations put forward by certain psycho-analysts (in particular C. G. Jung).

[2] Man's mental archetypes develop in consequence of an existential experience which puts him in contact with creatures, especially with

At this last point we limited ourselves almost exclusively to the supernatural archetype of bridegroom and bride, only indirectly touching on the problem of fecundity in terms of the interpersonal relationship of the partners. To be complete, a theology of the couple should embrace the husband as father and the wife as mother and attempt to illuminate this aspect of man and woman through supernatural archetypes of the same order as that of the bridegroom and bride. The ancient mythologies tried their best to do so by projecting, mistakenly, on to their divinities the sexual experience of the human couple with its limitations and defects – as if the archetype ought to conform in every particular to its earthly imitations, more or less distant,

other human beings, who are in reality images of God. As a result, they should bear some resemblance to the real archetypes of created beings, as they exist in God. But, on the one hand, since they result from an experience to some extent vitiated by sin and its consequences, they may distort more or less completely the model of which they are a reflection; on the other hand, they reflect only imperfectly supernatural realities, which it is impossible to know at the deepest level without a gratuitous revelation from God. Similarly, it is through my own father that I have an intimation in this life of the ideal Father, whose image I henceforth carry within me. My psychic life is thus preadapted to know God as Father. But to know him here and now in any effective way, as Father of men and Father in essence, I need the revelation which has its fulfilment in Jesus Christ. What is then the situation of a child whose deepest emotions have been scarred by its first contact with a brutal father? Such a child needs the authentic revelation of God the Father in order to correct the archetype of the Father automatically born of its personal experience. This example shows us clearly that there is a close correspondence, which it is important to emphasize, between the findings of psychology (especially depth psychology) and those of theology. The study of the language of Scripture, which is rooted in the human experience of Israel, is of great help in demonstrating this.

121

even distorted! Biblical revelation has a different view of things. But it is no less enlightening as regards the purpose of human fecundity and love, because it discovers their archetypes in the intimate life of God himself.

Even in the Old Testament God revealed himself as Father;[3] and the New Testament showed that it was not simply a question of metaphorical paternity or of an adoptive paternity with mankind as its only object: it was in fact an ontological paternity, which the mission of his Son here on earth revealed in all its profundity.[4] It is from this paternity that "all fatherhood[5] in heaven and on earth takes its title" (Eph. 3:15); and by this we should understand every parental relationship, of the father as well as of the mother, towards the children. It is true too that the rôle of the mother, in the mystery of Christ and the Church, is filled by the latter, the heavenly Jerusalem[6] (Gal.

O. Procksch, *Theologie des alten Testaments* (Gütersloh, 1950), pp. 503–12.

[4] C. Spicq, *Dieu et l'homme selon le Nouveau Testament,* pp. 47–108.

[5] For the meaning of the Greek *patria* in this context, see G. Schrenk in Kittel, *Theologisches Wörterbuch zum Alten Testament,* vol. 5, pp. 1019–1021; H. Schlier, *Der Brief an die Epheser,* pp. 167–8.

[6] The problem is more complex in the case of the mother in Apocalypse 12, whose first-born son is Christ (12:5). She almost certainly represents the human race, since with regard to Christ as well as with regard to us she fulfils a maternal function. This function in itself causes her to be considered a *new* humanity, shielded from the snares of Satan (12:6; 14:16). Cf. E. B. Allo, "L'Apocalypse" in *Études Bibliques,* pp. 176–8. It should not be forgotten that in fact the maternal function of humanity with regard to Christ has been fulfilled by Mary. The latter is therefore closely related to the archetype of the Mother presented in Apocalypse 12 and there is necessarily a very close connection between the mystery of the new humanity and the mystery of Mary. This is one of the funda-

4:26; cf. Isa. 54:1; 66:7–8; Ps. 87:5). God himself does not scruple to compare himself to a mother, when describing his love for redeemed mankind (Isa. 66:12–13). All parental love, even that of the Church, is nourished at the fountain-head of the divine paternity and our attitude of bride with regard to Christ should be accompanied by a filial attitude with regard to the Father, since by our union with Christ, the bridegroom, we become the sons of adoption in the Son by nature (Rom. 8:15–17; Gal. 3:26).[7]

Opposite this Father there is, however, no archetype of the mother, distinct from him, to bring the Son into existence. This does not prevent the mystery of interpersonal union, realized by means of conjugal love, finding its archetype too in God, under a different relationship: in the unity of the personal Spirit, the Father and Son are but one (John 10:30), and it is because they receive this Spirit that men have the love of God in them (Rom. 5:5), that they call him Father (Rom. 8:15) and become one spirit with the Lord (1 Cor. 6:17). This aspect of the mystery, which concerns both the intimate life of God and the participation in it granted to us, is not unconnected with the problem posed by the mutual love of husband and wife. This

---

mentals of Marian theology. It is notable that the Apocalypse does not succeed in co-ordinating perfectly the archetype of the Mother (Apoc. 12) and that of the Bride (Apoc. 21), both of which, nonetheless, refer to the same mystery of a new humanity. The mystery is seen in the two passages from different points of view.

[7] Here, too, symbols abound without any logical co-ordination. Several points of departure in human experience are needed to evoke a supernatural reality of another order: our relationship with the Father and the Spirit.

love aspires to mould them together in the concrete unity of *one flesh;* not in the sense that their personality would disappear, absorbed in a whole which would be superior to it; but in the sense that the personality finds its supreme fulfilment in communion and reciprocal giving. This is surely the meaning of human love. It must be added that this reciprocal gift of self has its normal fruition in a third person in whom the two others find the living symbol of their unity; nor is this without a parallel in the rôle which the Spirit fills with regard to the Father and Son: it is by his procession that their union is sealed, just as his mission here on earth seals the union of love between the Father and men, who have become his adoptive sons in the Son by nature.

In order to find for the human couple a final model whose characteristics they should imitate, we have to go as far as the intimate life of the triune God. It is true that the image does not slavishly copy its archetype and indeed would be incapable of imitating it in all its aspects. In addition, the mystery of Christ and the Church constitutes an intermediate archetype between this entirely transcendental archetype and the human reality which is its image, a link which recalls the rôle of Christ as mediator of revelation.[8] We must, however, keep in mind that the true function of the mystery of Christ and the Church

[8] The existence of this intermediate archetype is a reminder that revelation is not made up of abstract ideas relating to the mystery of God. It has been made accessible to men through actual concrete experience of the life of the Word made flesh. He is the indispensable link between the tripersonal God and ourselves, since the mystery of the covenant, in which God espouses humanity, is fulfilled in the real unity of his nature.

is precisely that of introducing men into the heart of the mystery of the Trinity. By participating in one, we also participate in the other. It follows naturally, therefore, that man and woman must model themselves on the couple Christ and the Church, if they want to imitate God who is Love (1 John 4:16). It is now easy to see the profound significance in the sphere of Christian revelation that the words of Genesis possess: "So God made man in his own image, made him in the image of God. Man and woman both, he created them" (Gen. 1:27). Not only have the human couple had from the very beginning a resemblance to God which makes them a mystery parallel to that of Christ and the Church (Eph. 5:32); but, through that very fact, the couple possesses the image of the living God, who is Father, Son and Spirit in a living unity.

It is in this perspective that we should place ourselves, before trying to evaluate the data on the subject of the couple provided by psychology (including depth psychology) and metaphysics, which are restricted by the bounds of purely rational examination and practised by men subject to error and to temptations of all kinds. The results of their investigations demonstrate in their own way both what the human couple is in the mind of God and what in the present condition of our race it has become through sin. But this evidence furnished in its raw state needs interpretation, for there is a great risk of confusing the couple "created in the image of God" and the couple fallen in the image of the protoplasts. It is not so easy to see man clearly: that strange mixture of animality, to some degree affected by neurosis and by spiritual aspirations which have no meaning outside a religious perspective, where man enters into a relationship with the living God. Left to themselves, man and

125

woman will always experience the insidious temptation to "become like gods" (Gen. 3:5) through the power of nature or rather through a hidden allegiance to the powers of the underworld, instead of having recourse together to the Unique Person who can make them divine by his free gift. Similarly, all human thinking on sexuality runs the danger of canonizing such a Promethean adventure in the name of reason, if it does not resort to the facts of revelation, expressed in the language of the Scriptures.

Once recourse has been taken to this source, everything falls into its proper place and a dialectic of love is revealed as beautiful and sublime as that glimpsed by Plato in the *Symposium*. The deep psychic injuries which attack sexuality in its vital powers and which psychoanalysis reveals, are no longer an enigma to which the key has been lost, for they have a place in the universe of sin and grace. The opposition which some people find between the tyranny of fecundity and the liberty of love or, on the other hand, between the nobility of procreation and the baseness of the instincts is seen to be artificial. The redemption of love by love itself, that secular aspiration of lovers which is impossible to fulfil at a natural level alone, is revealed as the supreme reality which underlies all human history, since this history is none other than that of a redeeming Love. Even the dream of paradise regained, on the canvas of which all human loves are embroidered, is no longer an illusion destined to founder in the void when man falls into the power of death:

We have not left the paradise of bliss where God first gave us place.

For, like its occupant, the garden is but blemished.

Its bounds are more impassable than fire, its calyx so finely
wrought

That God himself with us finds no way forth.[9]

---

[9] P. Claudel, *La Cantate à trois voix* (Cantique de la rose). It is through
the mediation of death that the widow Beata has discovered the eternal
presence of her dead husband. Here we have a telling symbol of Christian
redemption, as valid for the couple as for every human person: we must
die with Christ in order to be admitted with him once again into paradise
lost.